PORN
NATION

PORN NATION

CONQUERING AMERICA'S #1 ADDICTION

MICHAEL LEAHY

NORTHFIELD PUBLISHING
Chicago

All Scripture quotations, unless otherwise indicated, are taken from the *New American Standard Bible*, Copyright © 1960, 1962, 1963, 1968, 1971, 1972, 1973, 1975, 1977, 1995 by The Lockman Foundation. Used by permission. (www.Lockman.org)

All websites and phone numbers listed herein are accurate at the time of publication but may change in the future or cease to exist. The listing of website references and resources does not imply publisher endorsement of the site's entire contents. Groups and organizations are listed for informational purposes, and listing does not imply publisher endorsement of their activities.

Published in association with the literary agency of Sanford Communication, Inc., Portland, Oregon.
Cover Design: The DesignWorks Group
Cover Image: Jeff Miller / The DesignWorks Group
Interior Design: Smartt Guys design
Editor: Christopher Reese

Library of Congress Cataloging-in-Publication Data

Leahy, Michael.
  Porn nation : conquering America's #1 addiction / Michael Leahy.
    p. cm.
  ISBN 978-0-8024-8125-2
  1. Pornography--United States. 2. Internet pornography--United States. 3. Sex in mass media--United States. I. Title.
  HQ472.U6L43 2008
  176'.70973--dc22
                    2007048919

ISBN-10: 0-8024-8125-6
ISBN-13: 978-0-8024-8125-2

We hope you enjoy this book from Northfield Publishing. Our goal is to provide high-quality, thought-provoking books and products that connect truth to your real needs and challenges. For more information on other books and products written and produced from a biblical perspective, go to www.moodypublishers.com or write to:

Northfield Publishing
820 N. LaSalle Boulevard
Chicago, IL 60610

1 3 5 7 9 10 8 6 4 2

Printed in the United States of America

To Christine, my beautiful bride
and the love of my life

CONTENTS

PREFACE

WHAT'S *REALLY* GOING on HERE?

Six-term Rep. Mark Foley (R-Fla.) resigned amid reports that he had sent sexually explicit Internet messages to at least one underage male former page. Foley, who was considered likely to win reelection this fall, said in a three-sentence letter of resignation: "I am deeply sorry and I apologize for letting down my family and the people of Florida I have had the privilege to represent."

***

A football-loving 14-year-old boy with quiet parents pleads guilty to raping four primary school girls in a park in Salford, England. The forensic psychiatrist who examined the teenager said in court that the violent sexual images he had seen inspired him to carry out the offenses.

***

The Department of Homeland Security's deputy press secretary faces charges of using the Internet to seduce a detective he thought was a 14-year-old girl. The man sent the detective "hard-core pornographic movie clips" and used the chat room service "to have explicit sexual conversations," some of which the sheriff's office said "are too extraordinary and graphic for public release."

***

Police wondered where two girls, ages 11 and 12, who had posted photos of themselves nude on the Internet, got the idea. They said they were influenced by pornography on the Internet. Photos of the girls were downloaded and distributed at their school.

***

A Long Island man has been sexually abusing his 4-year-old daughter for almost her entire life—and recently offered to swap her for another child via an Internet chat room called "Baby Sex," police charged yesterday. The accused man, who lives in Dix Hills, was held in lieu of $1 million cash.[1]

We see the headlines and read the stories and shake our heads in disbelief, wondering, "What's going on here? Who would ever do something like that?" And then we read another. And yet another, the latter even more twisted than the first.

Some of us think to ourselves, "Wow, there are some really messed-up people out there. Sexual deviants that need to be locked up for good." Others reason that it's the porn industry and our hypersexual media who are to blame. They figure we're all becoming victims of a sex-saturated culture. Then there are those who insist poor parenting and centuries of sexual repression are the culprits behind our sexual pathology. Regardless of our own particular bias, we all tend to breathe a sigh of relief in knowing that we're not like them, and that they're not us. That it's just another news story about strange stuff that happened to someone else, matters far removed from our own personal lives.

But then you get the phone call from your sister-in-law with the surprising news that her husband, your brother, just announced he's leaving her and the kids for someone he met online. Or maybe she's the one who's leaving him for another man. Perhaps the stunning news was that of a longtime friend who's just been arrested and charged for soliciting sex with a minor.

Or maybe the newsflash hit closer to home and you're still reeling over the discovery of hundreds of pornographic images sitting on your family computer's hard drive. Graphic images and hard-core videos whose lurid titles and degrading file names betray their owner's best attempts to keep them hidden.

Again you find yourself asking, "What's going on here? Who could have done this?" But this time, there's a strong sense of urgency and importance you've never felt before. Because now, it's personal. No longer is it just a question of idle curiosity. The craziness you once thought only resided in other people's lives has just invaded yours. So you start looking for answers, searching for the truth. You have to know the truth because the stakes are higher now that you're involved.

But you're not the only one looking for answers. Because you're not the only one involved. There are others—spouses, sons and daughters, brothers and sisters, parents, coworkers, and friends. A web of people just like you who are trying to make sense of the offense or the abuse. And then there's the offender, or the abuser. You hope they're asking questions too, or at least asking for help.

"What were they thinking? How could they be so blind? What's *really* going on here?"

Speaking as one who's been both the offender and the offended, the abuser and the abused, questions like these have haunted me for most of my life. In my own case, as soon as I discovered that sex could make me feel better about myself, I gladly became a user. Whether it was trying to fix myself, to erase my pain and be "normal," or trying to cope with the stress and boredom of my everyday life, I used both porn and people, and kept secrets to hide my guilt and shame.

But then, I was caught. Exposed. The secret got out, at least part of it. But not enough of the truth came out, not enough to really break me. Before hitting bottom, the burning questions that kept me awake nights dealt more with how to keep hidden: "What if they keep digging, what if they keep searching? What will happen to me if the truth comes out? What will I do? How will I cope? What will I do to survive?"

It was only after losing everything that mattered to me—my fifteen-year marriage, my family of two boys, my home, my job, most of my friends, and my reputation in my church and in the community—that I finally hit bottom and began asking the only kinds of questions that really mattered: "How in the world did I get here? What was I thinking? How could I have been so blind?"

In other words, "What's *really* going on here?"

That was ten years ago.

That's when I started to write this book. Of course, I didn't know it at the time. All I knew was I needed to start somewhere. I had to discover the truth. The truth about me. So one day I sat down during my lunch break from work, pulled out a notepad, and wrote the title "The Truth about Me" across the top of page one. And I started writing. Then I stopped. Then I started writing again. And stopped again. Each time I'd start writing again, I'd look over what I had written before and I wanted to gag. Old lies, sugar-coating, people-pleasing prose.

It's now ten years since I began both my recovery and writing this book, and I'm just now beginning to realize how difficult it is for me to tell the truth about myself. The truth is, today, I'm a recovering sex addict. I've lived most of my life as a compulsive, pathological liar. That means I spent a lot of time covering up the truth. Granted, I haven't had to hide heinous crimes like robbing banks or stealing cars—my lies are far subtler, but no less destructive. Twisting the truth. Obscuring reality.

My battle in writing this book is that I'm trying to be honest, both with myself and with you, the reader. For some people who have been mostly honest all of their lives, this struggle may not make much sense. But for me, and I imagine for millions of others, perhaps even you, living out a life based on truth and honesty is a constant battle. So when we stop to look at the many sexual dysfunctions that are evident in our culture, we inherently know there really *is* something going wrong here. A lot of us have lived it in our own lives. It may not make the headlines, but we know it's there, recorded forever in the activity logs of our minds. We may have spent most of our lives running from it, or hiding from it, but we all realize that the truth about us is there also, battling the lies and crying out to be heard.

The battle of darkness and light that rages inside all of us is nothing less than a battle for freedom—your freedom, my freedom! My story is about the epic battle that has been raging underneath the veneer of my life. There are elements of this struggle that are universal to us all, and there are some that are uniquely mine. But at the end of the day, we have all fought our own skirmishes between the truth and the lie.

My hope for you as a reader and fellow sojourner is that you will recognize the signposts of your own life's journey in my story, and having seen a glimpse of what lies ahead, that you might seek out a straighter path to the freedom that awaits you.

INTRODUCTION

FACING
the TRUTH

It was almost too hard to believe. My suspicions had led to this—a suburban Atlanta address just a few miles from where I worked. I just couldn't get over how close it was. For almost a year now, Teresa said she'd been living back at home with her parents in Birmingham, and I had believed her. But this guy's name had kept popping up in our conversations, this guy in Alpharetta.

"A business associate," she'd say one day. Then months later, he'd be a family friend. And all those times she'd talked about the rush-hour traffic on Georgia 400 with frustration in her voice—why should she care? She lived three hours west of the Georgia 400. "I just know it's bad whenever I'm up there." Yeah, right.

But now that I'd matched his name to the local phone number she'd mentioned a few times, it was all coming together. And there it was on MapQuest, plain as day, only 6.2 miles away from where I worked.

"Oh no! No way! There's no way this is happening!" I jumped up from my office chair in a panic and grabbed the keys from my credenza, darting past the other offices without saying a word to anyone. The elevator seemed to crawl as I rode down to the building's entrance. I kept my head down as I blew by Debbie, the receptionist. I wasn't about to stop and chat with her, not now. As I hurriedly slipped through the front doors of our nondescript office building, a thought suddenly crossed my mind. *What if she's been lying to me all this time? What if she's living with another guy? This can't be happening!* I must have rehearsed those lines at least a hundred times in the few short minutes it took to drive to the neighborhood where my map address said he, and maybe she, lived. As I pulled up to the end of the cul-de-sac, I started checking the numbers on the black mailboxes. They all looked alike, very uniform, very suburbia.

Nice neighborhood, I thought to myself. And then I spotted it—house number 1516. That was it, the house I was looking for. I eased the car a little farther up the curb and parked alongside it in front of the neighbor's house. About then, I noticed my pulse was racing, quickened by waves of adrenaline.

I got out of the car and started up the driveway. It was quiet. No surprise. After all, it was close to noon and the kids from the neighborhood were all at school. I started to notice that I was breathing faster, feeling anxious. *I pray to God I'm wrong,* I thought to myself.

I quietly stepped up onto the red brick porch and began sheepishly peering through the front door's sidelight. It was midday and I had a hunch that she would be there. But no one was in sight. There were no cars in the driveway either. Maybe I was wrong. How could I have doubted her love like that? I started to feel like a fool, like an insecure and jealous boyfriend. I knocked on the door anyway. Silence. Just as I began to turn my head and start back down the steps, a woman suddenly appeared through the window sauntering from the kitchen to the den, cordless phone in hand. It was Teresa, standing there in a full-length white bathrobe, only ten feet in front of me. I stood there in shock for a second, staring at her through the narrow glass window. My stomach recoiled as if I'd just been hit by a sucker punch.

"No, no, no!" I started slamming my fist against the door as she peered back at me, acting surprisingly unconcerned about my unexpected visit.

"Teresa! Open the door! Open this door NOW!" As I waited for her to open the door, I watched her pace quicken. Still, she looked more concerned about ending her phone conversation than about what was to be the inevitable ending of our tumultuous two-and-a-half-year relationship. Then, without warning, a random thought interrupted my growing rage. Actually, it was a quote from the Bible, of all places.

You will know the truth, and the truth will make you free.

The placement of that thought was odd, considering what was going on. I was losing it, totally freaked to discover the woman I thought I loved walking around in her bathrobe in another man's house. I was enraged and I couldn't wait for her to open the door. I started thinking to myself, *Could I have been that stupid, that naive? Was I really that desperate for love, that blind to all of the obvious clues she'd left for me along the way?*

This woman, whom I had poured out my heart to, for whom I had sacrificed my marriage and my family, was not who she claimed to be. She was a lie. I banged on the door once again as she ended her phone call and started walking toward me, phone still in hand. With an irritated look on her face, she opened the door.

"Michael, what are you doing here?"

"What do you mean? What are YOU doing here?"

She started backing away from me as I burst into the foyer and continued raging. "How could you do this to me? You are such a liar! I can't believe you've been lying to me all this time, pretending to be with me while you've been living with someone else! Who is he? What's his name?"

In a measured tone, she tried to calm me down.

"Honey, this isn't what you think. He's just a friend."

"A friend! Yeah, right! You've been lying to me for nearly a year about living with a friend. I can't believe this! I can't believe I gave up everything for you!"

I don't remember much about our exchange after that. She started yelling back at me, and I continued raging at her. I was out of my mind with anger, yelling at her and yelling at myself and not believing my own ignorance, my own stupidity. At some point, I remember her telling me to leave and threatening to call the police if I didn't. That was just before I threw her down on the couch. The phone went flying out of her hand as I found myself summoning every bit of self-control I could to keep from hitting her. I'd never hit a woman before, but I could feel myself starting to lose it.

Before I knew it, the police showed up. She had dialed 911 just before I shoved her onto the couch. Apparently, the people at the response center could hear our argument and had wasted no time in dispatching a patrol car to check it out. Two officers decked out in their blues knocked on the door, and Teresa went to let them in. After splitting us up to ask us our own version of what was going on, one of the officers approached me once again.

"Here's the deal. She's not going to press charges." I remember my whole body freezing at the thought of how close I was to being arrested. "But you've gotta leave now. She wants you gone, and so do we. If you don't leave now, then we'll take you in."

"Don't worry, I'm out of here." I walked toward the door and headed for my car. I had no idea where Teresa was at the time. I never turned back to look, and I didn't want to. Suddenly, all I wanted to do was leave that place, and her, and never look back. I was in shock; I felt betrayed, used. I guess I had gotten what I deserved. This was exactly what so many people tried to tell me was going to happen.

I had sunk to a new low. Nothing like this had ever happened to me before. As I was driving away from that house and from the relationship that had started as an affair two and a half years earlier, I began thinking about what it had cost me: a fifteen-year marriage, my two wonderful boys, a promising family business partnership, and countless friendships. How could I have fallen in love with this woman? What had I been thinking? How had I let this happen? And how had I gotten to this point?

I found myself thinking about those words from Scripture once again, the words that had come to me as I had been standing at her front door: *You will know the truth, and the truth will make you free.*

In my arrogance, my first thought was, *Of course, now I know the truth about HER! I gambled on the wrong woman. She's the reason my life is a mess. She used me, lied to me, and deceived me. I'll bet everything she told me was a lie. I'll show her. I'm gonna blow her cover, make some calls, talk to some of her so-called friends she never would let me meet. I'm gonna find out the truth about her and throw it right back at her.*

The anticipation of vindication had never before felt so sweet, so just.

For the next several days, my life became "CSI: Atlanta." I was obsessed with trying to uncover every lie, reveal every affair, unravel every scheme I suspected she might have cooked up over the past several years. What I was really looking for was vindication, nothing more and nothing less. After all, my pride was at stake. It only took a few days and a dozen or so phone calls before the web of lies and deception started to unravel.

There was the lawyer in Montgomery, the couture shop owner from

Buckhead, the NASCAR driver from Charlotte, the stockbroker from Atlanta, the furniture salesman from Nashville, the office supplies business owner from Doraville, and the medical software sales rep from Atlanta whose house I had caught her living in. Then, of course, there was me. Most of us were married and had families when we had met Teresa. All of us were guilty of letting our lust hijack our sanity. But something deep down was telling me there was more to it than that. I wasn't sure what it was at the time, but I just knew there had to be something more. After uncovering unlucky guy number seven, I finally decided I'd had enough of the truth and gave up the search for more victims. It was becoming a pointless exercise in futility. The more lies I would uncover, the more I felt like an idiot and a blind fool. And then those all too familiar words came back to me again. But this time they took on a whole new meaning.

You will know the truth, and the truth will make you free.

Now I had grown up in a religious home and had spent enough time in churches over the years to recognize that this familiar phrase came from somewhere in the Bible. But beyond that, the words held little meaning for me. Even as I had been standing on that porch just days earlier, those words resounding in my head for the first time, the significance of their meaning had been lost on me in my moment of rage. But now, something about it was different. This time when the words came to me, I noticed that the emphasis had shifted in a way that gave this phrase a whole new meaning. I started to wonder if my earlier interpretation might have been wrong.

YOU will know the truth (about YOU), and the truth (about YOU) will make you free.

Huh? The truth about ME—not her?

This seemingly insignificant thought, confusing and brief as it was at the time, ended up marking a real turning point in my life. It was an epiphany of sorts, an intellectual and spiritual flash that would forever mark a change in the way I began to view myself and others. At a time when I found myself with no one else to lean on and no one else to blame, my focus began to shift as I started to hunger for the truth about me. This represented quite a change for someone who had been a pathological liar for most of his life. And this persistent little phrase—the truth about me—summed it all up for me at the time. My new mission in life was to discover what the truth about me really was.

As I started to examine myself and my life more closely, I came to realize that my circumstances weren't looking very good. Aside from the fact that I was able to find a well-paying job back in the computer industry after having been fired from my brother's business, I was pretty much facing life on my own. No one else really wanted to have much to do with me. That was hard enough. So the last thing I wanted to do was to set out on some inward-looking journey to discover the real truth about *me*. I didn't really like me too much at the time. In fact, I was growing sick and tired of myself as I wrestled with the guilt and shame of having abandoned my wife and kids for another woman. I had begun to spend more and more time using pornography and obsessing about sexual fantasies and less time investing in real relationships with real people.

"You will know the truth, and the truth will make you free."

The truth about YOU.

For the first time that I could remember, I truly felt hopeless and alone. The kind of alone that keeps you up at night wondering if you'll make it through another day. Wondering if anyone really cares about you, cares whether or not you're even alive. Everyone had left. Somewhere in the midst of my self-consumed arrogance and selfishness, they had all walked away. They'd had enough of me, and who could blame them? *I* didn't even like being around me anymore.

As I started to consider what it might mean to know "the truth about me," fear began to creep into my psyche, fear of what I'd find when I really looked deep within myself, fear of discovering who I really was inside and of learning what it was about myself that caused me to act out in a sexually compulsive way. I had spent most of my life avoiding these deep recesses of my heart. But now this fear kept creeping back into my conscious mind like an early morning fog, pulling me deeper and deeper into the darkness of depression as daylight faded into night. Suicidal thoughts started to reason with me as a more painless, albeit unattractive, alternative to the agony I was feeling. Oh, those dark and despairing nights! I was scared to death of spending the rest of my life all alone, unloved and unforgiven, and wallowing in the misery of my guilt and shame.

I was afraid to face the many questions I suddenly had about who I was and what I had become. But one question haunted me above all others. It was the first question I asked myself, and it refused to fade away. It was urgent and rather obvious, and it kept playing itself over and over in my mind, like a bad jingle that you can't seem to shake, no matter how hard you try.

How did I get here?

Somehow, I just knew that this was the starting point. This was the door leading to the way out. And if I wanted to rid myself of the misery that I alone had created, I had to summon what little courage remained in me in order to pursue the answer to that question. To discover the truth about myself, I had to face the truth about my past. I had to start at the beginning of my pain to find the birthplace of my lies.

PART 1

———

THE TRUTH
ABOUT ME

CHAPTER

1

LEAVING
PARADISE

B lue skies. Incredibly close, nearly touchable, warm blue skies. That's the first and last thing I think of when I think about growing up in southern California in the late '60s, when you could still see the sky in L.A. Living on the peninsula in a home perched high above the city, with panoramic views of an even bluer Pacific Ocean, was like living in a dream. It still romanticizes me to this day whenever I travel to L.A. Even when the valley is thick with smog, somehow when I look up toward the sky, my eyes only see blue.

Life was incredibly good back then—or at least as I recall. I was ten years old, the youngest of five, living in picture-perfect Palos Verdes, a new suburban enclave that was being carved out of the rolling hillside along the coastline just south of L.A. Sunsets were like elaborate production numbers filled with a rainbow of colors. Visits to the rugged sea cliffs were like Indiana Jones adventures, the rocks brimming with sea life. If you were bold enough to risk getting soaked by the white water of the crashing waves, there were always little surprises waiting to be discovered in the tide pools nearby.

Then there were the regular visits to the beach—soaking up the sun, body surfing, building sand castles. I even loved my school, where I was athletic and pretty popular and it felt like everyone was my friend. That was my life as a kid. "Leave It to Beaver" in Technicolor. I had it made! Life was good.

At home, everything was smooth sailing too. As the baby of the family, I was always well taken care of, looked after, coddled. I felt secure and safe. Our life back then was middle class with a forward lean into upper middle, thanks to my mom and dad's unapologetic affinity for a new concept called the credit card. We lived in a new home with a pool and a view of the Pacific Ocean. The real people of privilege lived a couple of miles away, on large ranches with acreage and in gated communities with romantic names like Rolling Hills Estates and Rancho Palos Verdes. But Sunmist Drive was enough for me. That and those amazing sunsets—exclamation points appropriately placed at the end of yet another perfect day in Paradise.

But that all changed one day. After gathering all six of us in the living room for an important announcement, I watched while my father, an overpowering figure in our home, strutted over to the stereo console to put a record on. The volume was turned up to the point that hearing him scratch the needle across the vinyl would make your heart stop. Next thing I knew, I felt like I was standing in the middle of a huge football stadium during half time with a hundred-piece marching band blaring out their school's fight song. My dad stood there with an expectant grin on his face, like the game show host for "Name That Tune," eagerly waiting for the next contestant to pounce on their buzzer and blurt out the right answer.

Then it struck me. This wasn't some lame home version of a faddish game show. This was our family tradition. "Name that college town and you've just learned where we're moving to next. Surprise!" I'd grown up hearing about this, like a family urban legend. I remember hearing my brothers and sisters talking about it. One day after school they came home to hear "The Eyes of Texas Are upon Thee" blasting through the windows of our suburban Chicago home, courtesy of the Texas Longhorn marching band. The next thing they knew, we were moving to Dallas. I was only one year old at the time, but they said it was all pretty exciting stuff. After all, Texas was bound to be much warmer than Chicago.

Five years later, it was a stirring rendition of the USC Trojan marching band playing "Fight On" that broke the silence of our tree-lined Dallas neighborhood. Before we knew what hit us, we were headed for L.A. Again, another standard of living and climate upgrade. I was six at the time, still too young to remember. But I'm sure we were all smiles once again.

Most major college fight songs were recognizable to us by now. That just went with being in a family of jocks where everything we did seemed to revolve around sports, especially football. But this latest rendition seemed to stump everyone. That meant we probably weren't going to recognize the city we were moving to, either. Maybe that's why everyone seemed a bit on edge. That and the fact that living in southern California wasn't just a dream to me, but it was Paradise to ALL of us. No one had ever considered that we might one day actually leave Paradise. After it was obvious that no one could guess the song, my dad broke the silence and spoke up in a confident voice.

"It's 'Bow Down to Washington!' We're moving to Washington!"

I think that was the cue for us to look and act excited. But this one I remember. I was ten, and I don't recall much excitement or happiness filling the room when the announcement came. It was more like a bad dream. It showed on our faces too. We were brokenhearted. No one wanted to move. No one wanted to leave Paradise. I could see my mom's eyes tearing up in the background. It felt like somebody had just died.

I remember breaking the silence at one point to ask my dad a burning question I had.

"Dad, where's Washington?"

I was pretty sure it was a long ways away on the opposite coast, somewhere near New York City.

"Washington's just up north of here a ways, son."

That was my dad, the eternal optimist and consummate salesman. He made it sound like it was just a few miles up the Pacific Coast Highway. You know, like we could just pop up there for the day and make it back to the beaches before sundown. That didn't seem so bad. But then the confusion started to set in.

"We're moving to Spokane, Washington."

What? What's a Spokane? It didn't sound right, and after he pulled out a map to show us where it was, it didn't even look like it was spelled right. I had enough of a challenge having to spell and pronounce my last name for everyone who asked: L-E-A-H-Y, like Lay-He. Don't tell me I'm gonna have to do the same thing every time someone asks me where I live—not Spo-KANE, but Spo-CAN. And I could see it definitely wasn't going to be a day trip getting there and back. A sinking feeling came over me. I didn't want to move to Spokane. I didn't want to leave Paradise. For the first time in my life, I remember feeling sad. Not just sad for a moment, but really sad—and confused.

Over the coming days and weeks, I was filled with a thousand anxious thoughts. *What about my friends? Does this mean I'll never see them again? And what about my school? And the beach? And my sea adventures exploring the tide pools at Abalone Cove?* The map showed that Spokane was a long way from the ocean.

My dad continued to give us his best sales pitch for a deal that was already done. With his eternal "can-do" attitude and fun-loving Irish personality, he was a master of the positive spin. Part dad, part motivational speaker. He grew up in Chicago, the youngest of seven boys in an Irish Catholic family full of outstanding athletes. He attended Western Michigan University where he was captain of the football team and eventually met and married my mom. A loud, warmhearted, blue-eyed Irish character, he still had a football lineman's physique left over from his years as a college athlete and Golden Glove boxer.

Dad was a gentle giant of sorts with an inherent goodness and a charisma about him that always put him at the center of attention in just about any setting. Like many of his generation, he started smoking and drinking while in the service. My mom would later confide in me that she thought drinking gave my dad the courage and self-confidence his tough-guy image otherwise lacked. It also gave him overconfidence and arrogance when he overindulged, which was a lot of the time as I recall. As a kid, I both feared and respected him. He was larger than life to me. He could kick my butt across the room when he felt like he needed to. And many times, he did just that.

I still had a lot of questions about this move. We all did. But that didn't matter. Before I knew it, the moving van was loaded up and we were on our way to Spokane. My mom started crying when she saw the Spokane Airport for the first time as we circled to land. A Quonset hut planted next to a long runway on the outskirts of town, this was a far cry from the newly opened Los Angeles International Airport we had just left behind. Pretty soon, my sisters were crying too. I was excited about flying, but really had no clue what I was in for. As soon as the freezing winter chill smacked my face, I started longing for my home, my friends, and those amazing sunsets. Having so many good memories made me sad. In fact, now that I think of it, *leaving* L.A. was the only bad memory I ever had of that place.

When we left southern California, it was Thanksgiving weekend and the weather at the beach was sunny and seventy-something degrees. When the moving trucks finally pulled up to our new home in Spokane, it was thirty-two below zero and there was two and a half feet of snow on the ground. I was quickly learning that Spokane was everything L.A. wasn't. But I was still yet to face the biggest changes of all. That would come only days later when I started going to my new school.

My parents enrolled me in a private school. It was the middle of the school year, and I was in the fifth grade. On my first day of school, I got lost walking home and nearly froze to death wandering the ice-packed streets of my neighborhood in subzero temperatures for hours looking for a house I hardly recognized. Not exactly a great way to start.

Things inside the classroom weren't much better. No one was impressed with my dark tan and beach blond hair, and I'm sure it didn't take them long to get tired of hearing me talk about how good life was back in sunny southern California. Spokane was surrounded by farms and forests, so my past was irrelevant to most of them. The school I went to seemed like it was filled with thugs and criminals, or so I thought. And the nuns and priests who ran the place acted more like wardens and prison guards than like the spiritually enlightened. I got pretty good at anticipating when a book or a chalkboard eraser would go flying through the air. Our teachers gave new meaning to the term "duck and cover."

It was here where I came face to face with my first "bully." Actually, there were several of them, and I seemed to attract them like a magnet. Being the new kid in school, my popularity was at an all-time low. I was threatened with being beat up and chased every day for months. In the process, I was also given a variety of unflattering nicknames that I still cannot bear to hear.

Then there was this guy who made a big deal of stepping on and smashing my bag lunch every day during recess in front of all my classmates. That went on for what felt like an eternity. Everyone laughed and thought it was hilarious. I was too embarrassed to tell my mom or dad or anyone else about it until one day a teacher walked in on the act. Nothing ever really happened to the bully, but it did put an end to the daily lunch "art" sessions. Of course, that would only give rise to other creative forms of harassment. I felt very alone and very different from everyone else while this was going on, and I didn't really understand what I had done to deserve it. I felt bad about myself a lot of the time, which was a new feeling for me.

At home, things weren't faring much better. Everyone's unhappiness with the move cast a negative pall in our home for some time. There were lots of tears and lots of complaining. I'm sure the move put a lot of pressure on my parents, especially on my dad since this whole thing seemed to be his idea. But in our family, it was always important to look good, to put on a happy face, even in the midst of sorrow or unhappiness. I did notice that my dad was drinking a lot more—or maybe he was drinking the same amount as before but now I was old enough to finally see it. Either way, it started really bothering me. Drinking never did appear to do my dad any good. For a brief period of time, it seemed to put him in the zone as the "life of the party." But eventually, the charm would wear off, and in its place was left a stupid, sloppy drunk. And when he was sober, he would often act the classic dry drunk—irritable, selfish, quick tempered. I wondered if I was the only one who could see this, the only one who cared. But at that time in my life, most of my brothers and sisters didn't seem to be around as much as I was to witness it firsthand. They were all older and spent most of their time away from the house with their friends or involved in other activities. And even when they were there, nobody ever dared talk about dad's "problem."

But over time, dad's problem increasingly became my problem. I learned that firsthand whenever I got in trouble, and those times seemed to come with more frequency the older I got. The worst times for me were the evenings, when I was up past my bedtime playing in my room. He'd notice my bedroom light was on, come charging into my room in a rage, get right in my face, and start yelling at me. The more booze I could smell on his breath, the worse I knew it would be. If I said the wrong thing or smarted off at him in response—or even said nothing at all—he'd start kicking me around the room like a football. Dad was built low to the ground, a former pulling guard in football with tree trunks for legs, so some of those kicks would literally pick me up off the ground.

My dad never hit me with his fists, but the kicking and the rage I would see in his eyes and hear in his voice were enough to crush my spirit every time. It was degrading, and it made me feel worthless and guilty, like I must be a bad person or flawed in some way to have deserved this. At the end of our episodes, he would typically add the caveat that "I'm sorry, but I only do this because I love you." I wanted to fight back, but I didn't know how. I was too young and too scared to fight back physically, so the thought never crossed my mind. In the end, I just wanted him to go away and leave me alone. But I loved him—he was my dad, my hero, the guy who protected me and kept me safe from whatever was out there in life that could hurt me.

I was thoroughly confused, so I learned to stuff the feelings I wasn't allowed to show that raged inside of me. I learned to keep silent, to bury the frustration and the confused feelings that I had. But now that things at home were getting as messed up as things at school, I started looking for a way out of my pain, a great escape. I wanted to feel safe and to be accepted once again—the way it was when we were living in Paradise. I longed to find some friends that I could hang out with, friends who would accept me the way I was. And I yearned to feel the joy and the happiness that I once had—anything to replace the pain that I was feeling by just being me.

CHAPTER

2

The
GREAT ESCAPE

The late '60s and early '70s were an awkward time to hit puberty, as if puberty itself weren't awkward enough. The sexual revolution was finally beginning to reach Spokane, and I was in the sixth grade, still facing my battles at home and at school.

I got involved in sports at school, so the bullying started to subside a bit. But I was far from being "one of the guys," an unfamiliar role for me compared to my life in L.A.

One day, on our school playground at recess, a group of bullies, the worst of the lot who had made sport of me for so long, were huddled together and were signaling for me to come join them. This typically was NOT a good sign, so I slowly and carefully moved toward them with fear and trepidation.

"Whaddaya want?"

"Come 'ere, we got somethin' we wanna show ya."

"What is it?"

"Just come 'ere! We promise we won't hurt 'cha."

I'd heard that promise before, but they seemed preoccupied with something they were all looking at. I moved up to the circle.

"What do you wanna show me?"

"Here, take a look at this! Whaddaya think?"

"It's a card. Queen of Hearts. So what?"

"No, stupid, turn it over."

On the back of the playing card was a picture of a woman. It showed her from the waist up. Naked.

"Sh-sh-she's naked! She doesn't have any clothes on!"

"Yeah. Pretty cool, huh!"

"Uh, yeah. Cool."

I was shocked. I'd never seen a picture of a naked woman before. But the first time I set my eyes on her, I could feel this rush of energy running through my veins. Like the rush of adrenaline I'd feel sometimes after making a big hit in football, only different. I liked the feeling. And my eyes really liked what they were seeing. Her beautiful form, her alluring smile. I just stood there staring at the card, mesmerized by the whole experience. I couldn't take my eyes off of her.

In the midst of my trancelike state, John, the group's ringleader, quickly snatched the card back out of my hand.

"Hey, don't tell anyone about this or we'll kick your butt. We could get in trouble, ya know."

"No, course not. Well, I gotta go. See you guys later."

"Yeah, later."

As I walked away, I could still see her picture in my mind. The look on her face and the way she smiled at me. Her shoulder-length, wavy brown hair. The shape of her body. It stuck with me like a photographic image with every last detail still intact.

And that adrenaline rush. WOW! What a feeling! As I headed back to class, I started feeling kind of guilty. After all, she was naked! And he said we could get in trouble for what we just did. But I also felt kind of edgy, even a little dangerous. I had been a part of something that was wrong, but I liked what I was feeling. Not just sexually aroused, something which at the time I didn't really understand, but I finally felt accepted, even if it was conditional acceptance based on the fact that I now had a secret to keep. My tormentors invited me into their twisted world, if just for a moment, and sent me on my way with a nod and a wink and a promise to keep. From that day on, my relationship with them changed. Granted, it wasn't the unconditional love and acceptance I was really looking for at the time. But I knew that my compliance with their demands for secrecy and sharing in their guilty pleasure with porn would make me part of the group. And because I knew things that could get them in trouble and didn't blow their cover, a trust was built. The bullying was over. No more harassment. No more rejection. Just keep this secret, and many more just like it, and the pain will go away.

Of course, I was elated to get these guys off my back. But I kept thinking back to that picture. Where do you find stuff like that? Over time, I'd find more pictures of naked women in the strangest of places. In the bathroom at some friends' houses. In the woods hidden under old pieces of plywood. In piles of trash. Whenever I'd see these pictures, I would gawk at them, drinking in the images. In the magazines, the pictures didn't just show women naked from the waist up. They were naked from head to toe, and in every shape and size imaginable. And unlike the black-and-white image on the deck of playing cards, these pictures were in color.

Most of the time I found *Playboy* magazines, but occasionally I'd stumble across some really weird stuff where men and women were naked together in all kinds of strange positions. I assumed they were having sex. I'd heard about sex before, but no one ever really sat me down and explained it to me. The magazines made it look pretty dirty, sometimes downright disgusting. The only sex education I'd had up until that point in my life was this special night class that the school I attended made my dad and me go to. It was taught by a priest. My dad said we were going to learn about "the birds and the bees." I had no idea what he was talking about.

We sat in a room with about thirty or forty other boys and their parents. They showed these gross anatomy pictures of male and female sex organs followed by diagrams where the man and the woman came together to make babies. It was painfully embarrassing to sit through, especially with all of your classmates and their parents sitting in the back of the room, including my dad. We just looked straight ahead and tried not to breathe or make eye contact with each other until it was over.

Later, on the drive home, my dad asked, "So, do you have any questions?"

Questions! Are you kidding me? I've got a million questions, I thought. So I responded appropriately for a kid my age.

"Nope."

"Okay then."

That's it. That was the extent of my formal and parental sex education. But soon after, I learned a whole lot about what it meant to be a sexual being. You see, looking at all of those pictures was exciting to me, but I still didn't know what to do with that sexual excitement until one day, down in my room, working on a class project for woodshop. We were learning how to use the lathe to turn wood and make stuff with smooth, round surfaces. The week-long class assignment was to make a lamp of your own design. We'd shape the wood in class on the lathe, then bring our lamp-in-the-making home with us to smooth down the rough surfaces with sandpaper.

One night, I sat on the edge of my bed with my two-foot-tall mahogany lamp clamped between my thighs, and started to rub it with sandpaper. After a while, I started to feel this strange tingling sensation between my legs. The harder I rubbed, the better it felt. Eventually, I felt this big rush. When I got up, I noticed the crotch of my pants was wet. I didn't know it at the time, but I had just had my first orgasm.

This was my accidental, if quirky, entry into the world of masturbation. Years later, my mom could never understand why I asked her to throw that lamp away when she found it while cleaning out the basement. Still unaware of the irony this iconic symbol represented in my life, she surprised me a few years after that by sending me pictures she had found of me as a proud artist unveiling his latest creation to the world, circa 1970. It still moves me whenever I see those photographs. On the one hand, I'm struck by the humorous irony of it all. Yet on the other, I'm amazed at how young and innocent I look in light of what I was learning about my sexual self at the time.

It didn't take long for me to make the connection between how looking at the pictures made me feel and what I experienced that night alone in my bedroom with a wooden lamp. I soon discovered that masturbating alone in my room, whether with real or remembered images of naked women, had an even more powerful effect on me. The sexual arousal leading up to a climactic orgasm would be like a thrill ride, putting me into an escalating state of excitement. Then, after I would climax, my entire body would fall into this trancelike state of relaxation. Sometimes I would even fall asleep. During the entire time, I could tune everything else out of my consciousness—past conflicts, present feelings, tensions and stress, even boredom—and simply concentrate on the pleasures of the moment. I could let my imagination run wild, putting myself in the picture or the image as the object of desire. Suddenly, I was accepted, desired, even loved—at least for a moment. And during those precious few moments, I was alive again in Paradise. No pain, only pleasure. I had found my Great Escape, a secret world that belonged to me and me alone. Short-lived as it was, I had found momentary joy and happiness again.

Throughout junior high, whenever I felt the tension and pain of life pressing down on me, I'd slip away to my bedroom or a bathroom and masturbate. Other times, I would do it in response to these new sexual feelings I was having, the sexual urge and frustration that come with puberty. The magazines and pictures were hard to come by, but it wasn't hard to pull up any of a growing library of images in my mind on demand. Of course, my growing desire for the material always demanded new images whenever I started getting bored with the same old stuff. But either way, this seemed to work for me whether it was to release the tension or relieve the boredom of my life. Unfortunately, it didn't really help me resolve the issues that were at the root of my discontent. My dad and I still clashed, only now as I got older, I started fighting back through disobedience and rebellion against his rules and his ways. That never solved anything, just like my Great Escapes never really changed anything about my circumstances except for how I felt at the moment.

Excluding that night my dad brought me to school to learn about the birds and the bees, most of the sex education I received through junior high came from either adult magazines or those friends of mine who also looked at adult magazines. There were very few references to sex on television, and most of that was through innuendo that sailed over my head. The sexual revolution started showing up mainly in the lyrics of our music and in television news reports about the free love movement taking place in faraway places like Haight-Ashbury and Berkeley, California. In Spokane, the sexual revolution was simply about having sex. There was that time in the eighth grade when I went out drinking with my friends and ended up in a park, rolling around in the grass with a girl I'd just met that night, my hand up her shirt. My buddies teased me about that indiscretion for a long time. Aside from that one fuzzy memory, I had never been with a girl before.

But that all changed in high school. Armed with adolescent ignorance and the raging hormones of a sophomore boy, I lost my virginity to a girl named Lynn who hung out with me and my friends. I liked her, and she was good looking, but I never really loved her. After taking her to a school dance, she invited me to come over later that week to a friend's house where she would be babysitting. That night we had intercourse. The whole experience was very surreal and very exciting to me, but void of any strong emotions. We only "hooked up" that one night. A few weeks later, I discovered that several of the guys I hung out with, including my best friend, had slept with her too. I was kind of disappointed, but not too much. After a while, we got tired of her and she quit hanging out with us.

That first experience best exemplified what relationships with girls were like for me in high school. We didn't call it "hooking up" back then, but that's what we did, with some degree of discretion. Lots of sex and one-night stands. I never really had a steady girlfriend in high school. I was too interested in being with a variety of girls, just like I saw in porn. In the world of pornography, the measure of a man was always based on how many women you slept with. Terms like "safe sex" and "AIDS" and "date rape" weren't in the vocabulary yet, and guys were clearly the sexual aggressors.

In high school I was a standout football player from a good family who had long hair, smoked and drank, and did drugs. That made me a hybrid of sorts with the ability to cross over into several large cliques. Even the teachers and administrators liked me—that is, when I didn't come to school high. I had a major meltdown with my parents during my sophomore year, when my drug use and rebellion was in full force. But I backed down, pledging obedience and promising to clean up my act as a condition of my not being sent to the Boy's Ranch, a local home for troubled teens.

Playing football again after sitting out my sophomore year helped me turn the corner. I quit smoking and cut down dramatically on the drugging and drinking so I could excel at the sport I loved the most. Throughout the rest of my high school career, my relationship with my dad improved markedly. In fact, my relationships with all of my friends and family got a lot better. I guess I started growing up a bit, and finally, I could start to think about going to college and getting out on my own.

College life fit me like a glove. I went to school at Eastern Washington University, a liberal arts school just west of Spokane. They were one of several colleges in the area who had recruited me to play football. I really wanted to go to the University of Washington, but my grades weren't good enough and I knew I wasn't big enough to play football in the Pac-8 (that was back in the day, before anyone acknowledged they also played football in the state of Arizona). So off to Eastern I went, and immediately I felt like I belonged. Our football team wasn't very good, and the seven thousand students there pretty much ignored us. But I loved to play the game, and I loved the camaraderie I had with the other athletes. College football players at any level are pretty much always on a testosterone overload, especially during the season. I was no exception. But add to that the sexual beliefs, attitudes, and behaviors that I had brought into college life, and mix in a healthy dose of autonomy and a total lack of accountability, and you could say that going to college was like pouring gasoline on my increasingly lustful desires.

Unlike my early days in a Spokane grade school where I felt rejected and all alone, I was in my element at Eastern. I played football for two years, then got tired of it and instead became involved in student government, where I excelled and was elected student body president heading into my senior year. I managed to make it through college without having a steady girlfriend, but also managed to stay sexually active right up until graduation. *Playboy* and *Penthouse* magazines were as commonplace in the dorms and houses where I lived as the student newspaper. And "hooking up" was no big deal, as long as nobody got hurt. Life was good, or so it seemed, and once again I was looking into the future with optimism. Because I had been able to maintain a 3.0 average while playing football and later serve as student body president, I had my pick of several blue-chip corporations to go work for after graduation. I chose IBM Corporation in spite of the fact that I knew nothing about computers. It just sounded like a good place to work and make a lot of money, something that was definitely in short supply throughout my college years.

In June of 1980, after giving the commencement speech to my graduating class and several thousand onlookers, I piled everything I owned into the back of my car and headed down I-90 toward Paradise once again. I was going to spend the next two weeks in California, revisiting the places of my youth that I had left behind twelve years earlier and not seen since. I went down with a strong sense of pride and accomplishment. I had made it through college and I had a great job with IBM waiting for me in Seattle when I returned. It would be a new life, a good life, and the future looked bright.

Meet **KEN & BARBIE**

Returning to California to visit the place of my youth taught me an important lesson—you can never go back. Everything had changed dramatically in just over a decade. Our old home in Palos Verdes had become prime real estate and was now worth ten times what we paid to have it built. All of the old neighbors were gone. Even the school looked different, and no one there remembered who I was. But I could still recognize that blue sky and those incredible sunsets. That alone made it well worth the trip back.

The early '80s was a good time to live in Seattle. It was an even better time to work in the computer industry. Between my job, spending time with my family, and indulging in the Seattle night life in the early days of punk rock, I kept myself pretty busy. Of course, making new friends took a bit more effort than it did in college, where I spent all four and a half years living on or near campus. But then again, there were the bars and after-work happy hours. I didn't slow down much from my partying ways in college, and a prime objective for me was to finish the night in bed with some woman, any woman. I quickly learned that wearing a suit and tie and having an IBM business card was great bait for attracting women. I spent most Thursday, Friday, and Saturday nights out drinking and cruising the nightclubs with my friends. We were all looking to score.

Sometimes, if no one else wanted to go out, I'd go it alone. Getting a woman to go home and sleep with me was like closing a big sale, or making that big hit in football. There was a similar high, a similar buzz compared to what I felt when I masturbated to porn, only this was a real person. But since it was almost always a one-night stand (I would seldom call them the next day, and often couldn't even remember their names the next morning), having anonymous sex was like a step up from porn without the complications of having a real relationship. I left it up to her to protect herself from getting pregnant, but didn't really care much one way or the other since I knew I'd never see her again. Occasionally I'd ask a woman out for a second or a third date, but that was usually because I knew she'd have sex and I didn't want to have to expend the effort to find someone new that day.

It was in the midst of this sex-driven existence that I met the woman who would soon be my wife. Her name was Patty, and we literally ran into each other one night as she was coming off the dance floor and I was headed to the bar for another drink. I was in Atlanta attending an IBM training class, and as usual I was out trolling the bars with my classmates, looking for bodies overboard. She was just standing there, Southern accent and all, and I jumped at the opportunity before me. I immediately asked her to dance, and we stayed on the dance floor for the next several songs. When the friends she was with told her they were leaving, I promptly asked if I could call her and take her out to dinner. She said yes and gave me her phone number. Things were progressing exactly according to plan.

Our first date was just a few days later. We sat in a restaurant and talked for nearly four hours and I honestly don't remember thinking much about sleeping with her. She was smart and engaging and very opinionated. And I could see she had a good heart to go along with her wit and personality. We didn't talk for about a month after I returned to Seattle. Then, out of the blue, she called me. That was really when things got rolling. The next few months consisted of marathon phone calls between Atlanta and Seattle, trips to Atlanta, and a trip or two for her to visit my family and friends in Seattle.

When I first met Patty, she was what I would call a conservative Southern Baptist, much like my dad was a conservative Catholic. My mom and I were a bit more liberal leaning in our views on God and faith. Family and faith were very important to Patty, so a lot of our early discussions centered around our belief in God. Even though I stopped going to church as soon as I left home for college, I could still talk the talk pretty well.

"Of course I believe in God. Sure, I have a Bible. Oh, yeah, I read it all the time." Lies, lies, lies. *But hey,* I reasoned to myself, *I'm a great guy and I'm Irish Catholic and I even attended a Catholic grade school for eight years and was an altar boy. That's gotta count for something. Plus she would be such an amazing catch. So what if I stretch the truth a bit? After all, this could be the biggest, most important sale of my life.* Of course, I didn't go into great detail describing what my sex life had been like, and I never told her about my affinity for pornography.

I convinced myself that we were a good match, and that our sexual pasts weren't important. And I reasoned that once we were married, I wouldn't want to look at that stuff anymore. Somehow I just knew that my lust for the material would magically go away once we started having regular bedroom sex as husband and wife. But just to make sure, right before I asked her to marry me, I took a trip to a place called Hedonism with a couple of my friends for a final sex binge. Let's just say that the resort lived up to its name, and leave it there. My goal was to get it all out of my system so that I would be ready to settle down to a wife and, hopefully, a family of my own. Funny how feeding your addictions in no way gets them out of your system—funny.

The following November, just over a year after we first met, Patty and I got married in her hometown of Savannah, Georgia. I remember that there were a lot of people I didn't know who showed up, even in our wedding party. We had both a Catholic priest and a Baptist minister presiding over the wedding ceremony. Afterward, a bunch of people jammed into the rec hall of a nearby middle school for the reception. As I glanced over at Patty through the din of the music and talking and laughter, I suddenly realized that my life was about to change. As I stepped outside myself (as one does at such moments and events), assuming the objective viewpoint of narrator, I declared to myself that this was to be a defining moment of my life after which nothing would be the same. And I truly believed me. Patty had just become my wife. I was happy and hopeful of a great and long life together.

But the first clue suggesting my past was not getting boxed up along with my bachelor furnishings came no sooner than on our actual wedding night. While Patty and I were hanging out in the lobby of the hotel, I started having a few drinks with my family and friends. As the night wore on, I started noticing the other women in the lobby, drinking in images as I used to with pornography. Part of "drinking in images" involved undressing them with my mind, followed by imagining myself having sex with them. It's a form of mental rape and is sexually arousing in a way that can hardly be detected by anyone else. It was a way of feeding myself lustful thoughts to fantasize on later.

So here I was on my wedding day, Patty all dressed in white, yet all I could think of was having sex with some of the bridesmaids and barflies at the hotel pub. Later that night, when Patty and I were finally alone, I would tell her that I was too tired from the busy day, then roll over and fall asleep. I never gave a second thought to what this night meant to her, and what kind of memories she would hold on to from that day. In retrospect it was ironically poetic: as the wedding night is the unveiling of one's spouse, Patty had gotten to see the real me as well as a trailer for the next decade and a half of our marriage. Nearly fifteen years would pass before we would ever talk to each other about what didn't happen on our wedding night and many other nights to follow.

The next clue things might go wrong came on our honeymoon. More of the same. I couldn't keep my eyes off anything female sunbathing, swimming, lying, or walking. I tried my best not to let Patty see the double takes, as if women don't know when you're checking out other women. The continual fantasizing led to the atrophy of my sexual desire for her, which was crazy because we were still newlyweds. But she was only one woman, and there is one thing that one woman can never provide . . . the endless variety that porn provides. Not long after we got back from our honeymoon, we settled into our new home in Seattle. No sooner was our honeymoon over than our sex life started on a steep decline. Yet my sexual appetite was steadily growing.

Within our first year of marriage, I was back to using pornography on a regular basis. Once again I had something to hide as I took my sexual habits underground. Over the next several years, Patty and I settled into our routines as a couple. A year and a half into our marriage we moved to Atlanta, and shortly thereafter our oldest son, Christopher, was born. Patty stayed at home from work for the next six years to care for Christopher while I worked in sales for an assortment of computer companies. My jobs always paid well but came with a caveat. Being in the technology industry in the late '80s–early '90s, I had easy access to a rapidly growing library the porn industry was delivering to consumers through emerging technologies.

Back in the late '70s, pornographers took a gamble and made a technological leap away from the more expensive film production processes and started shooting their movies on the lower-cost VHS video format. This gave them ready access to the homes of average Americans who were buying up VHS cassette players by the millions. I snuck a number of X-rated videos home myself when they first came out, but I was uncomfortable renting adult videos from the neighborhood video store for fear of being seen by someone I knew.

It was a similar story with adult videos on cable TV. Once again, a new means of content distribution had been developed that could bring porn right into the homes of millions of Americans. But it would have been impossible to unblock the Playboy channel or hide the charges on our cable bill in a way that Patty wouldn't see it. So I steered away from such risky ventures, settling instead for a late-night peek at a breast here and a leg there on the "fuzzy channel"—scrambled cable channels with adult content that weren't so thoroughly scrambled after all. I would wait for Patty to go to bed before changing channels. Understandably, my habitual coming to bed late at night would frustrate and anger her, only inflicting more damage to our already stifled sex life.

But the big opportunity for me, which meant a big setback for Patty's and my relational intimacy, came with the advent of the Internet. I first started using the Internet while at work years before the average consumer had ever even heard of it. All of us who worked in the tech industry got our hands on the first generation of high-resolution porn, first through CD-ROM technologies and later through the Internet itself. Suddenly, it was as if my world changed overnight. Now I could have access at work over high-speed connections to hundreds of Web sites, each showing hundreds of high-resolution pornographic photos.

In a matter of a few short years, those hundreds of sites multiplied into thousands, then tens of thousands. And the number of photos per site multiplied as well. Then there were links to other sites, and pretty soon videos were being added to the vast libraries of photos.

The biggest change the Internet brought about was that I could now indulge myself in surfing through thousands of movies and photographs for hours on end and remain totally anonymous. That is, until the companies I worked for started figuring out why their network capacity was rapidly disappearing and they started monitoring Internet use. But those days were still far off for me. I was an early adopter of this brand-new wide world of entertainment, and I dove in head first like a kid in a candy store, only I knew I could indulge and remain totally unseen and anonymous.

By this time, Patty had given birth to our second son, Andrew, after nearly seven years of our struggling through the emotional ups and downs of in vitro fertilization. By now, our sex life was on life support and barely alive. Yet as far as our family and friends were concerned, we still looked like the picture-perfect couple. In fact, after moving into an upscale neighborhood in the northwest suburbs of Atlanta, the neighbors affectionately referred to us as "Ken and Barbie." In their eyes, we had it all—a beautiful home, wonderful kids, great jobs, new cars, and good health. But what they couldn't see was the hidden cancer that had been slowly, methodically eating away at our marriage and threatening the survival of our family since long before our wedding day.

What no one could see, not even Patty or the boys, was that I was starting to lose control of my secret world. The lies that I had neatly tucked away, year after year, were starting to come undone as my life became increasingly unmanageable. I had crossed a line some time ago where my hidden sexual habits had turned into sexually compulsive and addictive behaviors. It was just a matter of time before the bomb would go off and the truth would finally be known. How or when or where was yet to be determined, and I was oblivious to the danger that lay ahead. But the outcome was inevitable. The truth was, I couldn't stop. I wouldn't stop. And I was going under fast.

CHAPTER

4

GOING
UNDER

Pornography and masturbation had been a part of my life for over two decades. We had a relationship, an understanding. It was give-and-take, but I always felt that I was in control, that I could manage it. Of course, I was just deceiving myself.

The dependency I had built up over time and the expectations I had on my Great Escape's ability to help me cope with all of life's twists and turns were simply unrealistic. My use of porn was never stagnant. It was dynamic and ever changing, just like the medium itself. It ebbed and flowed. At times I could take it or leave it, and at other times I needed it and had to have it. But there were two key limiting factors that had kept my use of the material in check. Those were the lack of availability (or accessibility) and anonymity.

But the Internet had smashed through both of those barriers. I could now access any images I wanted, tapping into new genres or categories of porn that I never knew existed before. And I could do it all instantaneously and anonymously. The stealth factor was perhaps most important to me because I needed to keep things hidden. My habits needed to remain out of sight from others, especially Patty and the boys, if I was going to continue to use. The Internet allowed me to fly under the radar while actually increasing my consumption of the material. I thought I had it made, especially since I was a tech industry insider with high-speed Internet access. I was the wolf guarding the hen house, and all I needed to indulge my senses was more time.

That time was granted, but at the expense of time spent with my wife and family. It started off with using while on business trips—time that I figured was already mine away from family. I thought as long as I was traveling on business, I wasn't really cheating them. But I was, not to mention stealing time from my employer. I would add a day or two here and there to my travel plans, stretching them out beyond necessity for the express purpose of creating more time to act out sexually.

While traveling on business, I was on my own and accountable to no one. As long as I took care of business, the pleasures I would indulge in—on pay-per-view cable movies and undisturbed time cruising the Internet—were well deserved, or so I reasoned. But I convinced myself that I deserved it. Eventually, that practice caught up with me in the way of subpar sales performances and having a higher cost of sales than my peers, two factors that led to my inability to hold a good sales job for more than two years.

The humiliation that I would feel losing job after job and lying to my wife and kids and friends about the reasons just acted to heap more guilt and shame on my shoulders. I was a good salesman and certainly had the list of impressive corporations on my resume. I sold my curb appeal to others like a master of his craft. But when it came time to do the work, my loyalties were always divided. Losing jobs created more stress and financial problems, which propelled me back into my Great Escape as a way to numb the pain of the consequences. But it wasn't enough to get me to stop. I just kept going back. Lust had become a relentless taskmaster, and I was enslaved to it.

The more time I had to myself, whether employed or not, the more time I spent indulging in porn. Now fast access was becoming available at home. But there was another factor at play here that led to an escalation of my growing addiction. Having access to a broader variety of genres, or categories of images, I started exploring the steamier side of porn out of sheer curiosity. Stuff I had only heard of or never even knew existed before—group sex, S&M, girl on girl, Web cams. There were literally hundreds of niche categories to explore, and I was hungering for more.

One in particular, voyeurism, caught and held my attention. I don't know exactly why. Maybe it was those ads in the back of *Boys' Life* magazine for X-ray glasses that captivated my imagination as a child growing up. The thought of being able to see through women's clothes and see them naked, just like the ad depicted, was exciting to me back then. I guess it was still exciting to me as an adult because voyeur Web sites had a special attraction for me. I'd spend hours pouring through site after site, Web page after Web page, looking at hidden camera images of unsuspecting women who were photographed while they were undressing, or taking a shower, or standing naked in the bathroom while putting on makeup, or using a tanning bed. The fact that most of these pictures, if they weren't staged, were a criminal violation of a person's right to privacy never seemed to matter much to me at the time. All that mattered was that it gave me a higher high.

My "connection" with this particular genre of porn somehow created a higher level of sexual stimulation for me. Over the years I had unconsciously created a hierarchy of needs based on sexual stimulation that had a direct impact on how much pleasure I would experience when looking at porn.[1] For instance, it was more stimulating for me to see hidden camera shots of an unsuspecting woman getting undressed than it was to look at group sex pictures, which was more arousing than heterosexual sex, which was more exciting than pictures of a naked woman posing alone. But whenever I used these edgier images, my sexual arousal and the resulting climax was more intense.

Once I figured out that I could get a higher high and zone out even more by using hard-core porn as my drug of choice, I started spending more time exploring darker genres of images. The more disturbing the image, the more I found I had to separate my relational emotions and values from what I was looking at and view the women as objects instead of people. That was the only way I could reconcile what I was doing with these images in my mind. Even though they were only images, I still found I had to separate or dissociate my emotions from how I was "using" these people for my own gratification. Otherwise, I couldn't cope with my own repulsive thoughts about myself and what I was actually fantasizing about doing. The more I went there, the more I started hating myself for who I was as a person.

What I didn't realize at the time was that this would somehow transfer over to the way I treated real people in relationships in the real world, especially women. My objectification and sexualization of women in porn became objectification and sexualization of the women I had relationships with in my life—including Patty. In time, I started caring less about others and more about what I was getting out of the transaction, a characteristic of objectification. This led to my spending less and less time with Patty and the boys and even friends and family since my interactions with them were increasingly at the cost of my time spent with porn.

Real women like Patty were no match for what I was getting from porn. Porn didn't ask questions, never complained, and had no needs for me to meet. It was always there, waiting on me hand and foot, ready to meet my sexual needs on demand, whether that meant blonde or brunette, big or small, one-on-one or with a group. Whatever I wanted, whatever I demanded, in the back of my mind I knew I could always count on the Great Escape to deliver.

What I didn't count on was how hard it would be to stop. I guess it's because I never really wanted to stop. Even though every action was being influenced by my thinking about how I was going to satisfy my sexual appetite that day, I still felt like my life was manageable and under control. I had my limits and set my boundaries. Porn was the limit—no hookers, no strip clubs, no massage parlors or one-night stands—just porn.

Then one day, during a business trip, I found myself in a hotel room looking out my window and I spotted a woman in another room with the curtains slightly open. I could see her undressing. Immediately, I began feeling a rush. I started trembling as my pulse quickened. This was much better than looking at porn. *This is real*, I thought. *And I can enjoy the show without ever having to leave my room. Little threat of being seen by others too. I'm just looking through my window across the courtyard, not creeping around outside peeping into other people's rooms.* This rationale suited me just fine. I reasoned that it was her fault for leaving the curtains open.

In spite of my justification, I had just crossed a huge line. I had moved from acting out on pictures to acting out on people themselves. It was the greatest of all the Great Escapes as I began to watch and satisfy myself while these reality-porn dramas would slowly unfold outside my hotel windows. Of course, engaging in this type of voyeuristic activity required massive amounts of time. Three, four, five hours at a time just standing there looking out my window was not unusual, and almost always this would continue into the late night and early morning hours. Nothing else I had ever done even came close to arousing me the way this did. I had crossed a line, but I had also reached a new level of sexual stimulation, and I knew there was no turning back.

That's how it works. That's how you lose control. You cross boundaries, step over the line, exceed the limits that you set for yourself while trying to stay in control. But to do that is to deny yourself the greater pleasures and higher highs that you aspire to. For me, stepping over the line and going from looking at voyeurism Web sites and images to being one in real life was a huge leap.

Along with the higher highs, I found that my shame and guilt intensified as well. The higher I would rise, the further I would fall afterward. I started really hating myself and what I was doing. My actions were creating chaos in my mind and acting like a cancer to my soul. When I would spy on a real woman getting dressed or undressed, the shame and guilt of realizing that I could have been arrested for what I had done confirmed in my mind that I really was a bad person, that I was a sexual predator who just hadn't been caught yet. No better than those guys you see on TV getting busted for peeping or indecent exposure. Every time I gave in to this darker sexual urge, there was a newer, greater pain to soothe, a self-inflicted wound that I needed to medicate, but now with stronger, more potent medicine. And I knew exactly what would do the trick—for the moment. The resulting shame and guilt and self-hatred I felt after acting out yet again would pull me back down and motivate me to act out once more. It seemed never ending. I was caught in an addictive cycle that was spiraling out of control and ever downward.

At this point in my life, I had become totally self-absorbed. Patty and I were acting more like roommates than husband and wife. I was spending little time with either her or my boys as I was consumed with trying to manage the unmanageable. There was little intimacy left in our marriage, and our relationship revolved around accomplishing the everyday tasks of running a family, of which she now carried the bulk of the burden. My sexual acting-out behaviors were getting riskier and riskier as simply viewing porn didn't do it for me anymore. I started to spend more time fantasizing about being with other women, with real women, and started obsessing about having an affair.

During a high school class reunion, which I went to by myself, I ran into an old girlfriend of mine. Our exchanges at the reunion were innocent enough. We were both married, she with five kids, me with two. But after returning home from that weekend away, reminiscing with her about old times, we started sending each other e-mails. The dialogue became quickly rooted in fantasy and eventually became sexual in nature. It was just another line crossed. Not a physical affair, but certainly headed toward an emotional affair. By now, I was an affair just waiting to happen.

That opportunity came in late May of 1997. I had left the computer industry to "take a break" after cycling through one job after another. My brother and his partner had a growing business and were looking to expand, so I convinced them to open up a branch office in Atlanta and I became its general manager.

One day, I had an appointment with a prospective customer who was about to place a large order with us. She pulled up in a late-model red Mercedes convertible. Her name was Teresa, a tall blonde woman in her late twenties and dressed to kill. The guys in the shop and in the front office stopped what they were doing to gawk at her as she strolled toward my office. We had talked several times before over the phone but had never met face to face. There was a lot of playful flirting during those phone conversations, and each time I hung up I would fantasize about what she looked like and what it might be like to have sex with her. But what I saw that day walking into my office exceeded all of my expectations.

In a word, she was hot. She had a steamy, sensual look about her that wasn't what I would call beautiful, but was very sexy to me. She looked to me like porn with skin on. The way she dressed, the way she talked, her body shape and size, her mannerisms and personality—she was the epitome of what I had been searching for in porn all those years. The personification of porn. The more we talked, the more connected I felt to her. And her come-ons didn't go unnoticed by myself or the others. By the time she left our office, the guys were talking about how hot she was and how she was hitting on me. I knew it too but tried not to let on to the others. If anything was going to happen between us, it needed to be in secret. But just the thought of us hooking up had my pulse racing.

After just a few short weeks and several more meetings, I found myself alone with her in her apartment. I had offered to stop by to get her signature on some orders, but by then we both knew what our real intentions were. That day we had sex for the first of what would be many times spent together. During the first several months of the affair, I was in constant contact with her by phone, pager, cell phone, and e-mail. It was typical for us to communicate with each other up to a dozen or more times a day. And with each phone call or page, my pulse would quicken and my heart would start to race. I knew what we were doing was wrong, and that if I ever got caught it would surely spell the end of my marriage. Patty's feelings about cheating were made crystal clear to me before we were married. But I was hooked on the high. It was scary and dangerous and exciting, a 24/7 rush of adrenaline. I would start to feel doped up just thinking about it and secretly planning for our next illicit rendezvous.

Even after confessing the affair to Patty a few months after it started, I didn't really want to leave it. Patty had suspected something was going on and confronted me by asking me if I was having an affair. Very matter-of-factly, I said yes. By then, I was so filled with arrogance that I just wanted to get it out in the open and continue to pursue this fantasy dream girl. But then I noticed Patty's reaction. It was as if I had clubbed her in the stomach. Her response was immediate shock, and then violent anger. Eventually, when the police showed up after the neighbors complained about all of the yelling going on next door in the middle of the night, she was chasing me around the room, clubbing me with a plastic baseball bat. Thank God it was only plastic. Her anger and rage and shock frightened me with their unpredictability. Had there been a gun in the room, I'm not sure I would have left there that night alive. Afterward, I felt lower and more despicable than ever. The next morning, totally exhausted and emotionally drained, we sought outside help from a counselor. But the chaos that would become our lives had only just begun.

For the next year and a half I promised Patty and counselors and therapists and pastors and myself over and over again that I would stop seeing Teresa. But over and over again I broke those promises. I was addicted to a relationship with porn with skin on now, and I found that I just wasn't willing to walk away. The months and months of compulsive lying and betrayal that followed were devastating to Patty and the boys. Our families were also deeply disturbed to see our marriage and family disintegrate right before their very eyes. I appeared to be in a fog and unreachable by everyone who tried to help, and there were plenty of people who tried. But the fact was, I *was* unreachable. I was living in a cloud of arrogance and self-righteousness, isolated and in denial of the fact that I needed help. There were the occasional rescue efforts and interventions designed by well-intending family members and friends. But I didn't really want their help. After all, I still believed that I had everything under control.

If I could have "had my cake and eaten it too," I would have. That would have meant having both Patty and Teresa in my life, both fighting to meet my needs, and that is the way it was for a time. But it came at a steep price. For Patty and the boys, it did untold damage and nearly cost Patty her life as she contemplated suicide while in the midst of this battle to save her marriage and family. It almost cost me my life as well, as Patty would later disclose an incident where—my back turned to her—she fought back the powerful urge to take the kitchen knife she was holding and thrust it into my spine. Eventually, it did end up costing me everything.

While my life was free-falling in a downward spiral, there came a time when Patty and I decided to free ourselves from each other. I knew if I cut her loose, she could return to the surface to try to pick up the pieces of her and the boys' shattered lives. It was never an option during our fifteen-year marriage to consider divorce. But at some point in the midst of this battle that now pitted me against them, it became obvious to us both that this would be a battle to the death—either hers or mine or one or both of the boys, likely by suicide. Cutting them loose was probably the only humane thing I did for my family during our last eighteen months together. I was otherwise unremorseful and unrepentant and left Patty with a shattered heart after squeezing every last bit of love she had for me out of it. The boys quite simply had lost their dad. Few things in life could have devastated them more.

This is my vantage point, but there is another perspective, one that every woman has and every woman fears. And no story like this one would ever be complete without telling it from her point of view and in her own words.

CHAPTER

5

In
HER OWN WORDS

A fter I confessed my affair to Patty, she began to keep a journal. She would later tell me that putting her feelings and emotions and experiences down in writing was a cathartic process for her from the very start. It also says in a raw, unedited form what I could never say about how my sexual addiction affected her and our two boys.

This is not a chronology, nor is it a complete record of all of her journal entries. These random excerpts are merely a sampling of the inner turmoil Patty dealt with during the worst of our times together. Her writings became letters to God and to herself and undelivered letters to me. As such, they speak for themselves and require no further commentary.

***

Michael,

I feel all we do is argue over you being late. Or should I say—you say one thing and you always do another. You want me to trust you but how does one <u>trust</u> a person who _never stands_ by his _word_—that is really a tough one for me to handle. It may not seem important to you but to me especially right now—I am trying to develop a sense of trust but you make it tough. Please be more respectful to me. It isn't about you being at work late, it's the principle of the issue.

***

God,

Confused—brokenhearted—disappointed—scared—unsure about myself—rejected—where is my life going? I can only see the small picture—I know you see the big picture and what is best. Lord I love you—please hear my prayer.

***

Dear Journal,

Does Michael love me like he used to—our relationship has been tainted—will things get back to normal? Does Michael think of only me when we are _making love_—this probably haunts me the most—I hope he only sees me—I will never truly know—time is our best friend! I miss the innocence of our 1st years of marriage ... Michael so strong— yet he needed me—does he need and really want me now?

***

Dear Journal,

As I was riding today from Savannah to Atlanta I realized how alone I felt in trying to handle all of the information I have heard about my husband of 13 years. What I have learned most about the entire ordeal and have been through since July 11 is that communication is so key to a healthy and happy marriage. Michael and I had been really acting more like roommates than husband and wife. With two children involved 2 yrs. and 10 yrs. and our oldest son involved in every sport during the year we did not seem to find any time together. I let my schoolwork, neighborhood tennis, my children all come 1st in my life and somewhere at the bottom came Michael! We had spurts in our marriage that were great sexually but for the most part I had a really hard time showing my passion and love for my husband! I am not really sure why this happened. I have a lot of theories but there is no one to blame but myself. I blame myself because I did not express this to my husband for years. I feel badly for Michael—"cold dead fish," that was what it was like being in bed with me—not always but a large part of the time. Michael also did not communicate his desires to me—I thought he did not have much of a sex drive or I just did not do much for him—as boring as I was I am sure I did not exactly make him want to drop his pants and make love to me on the countertops.

***

Dear Journal,

Feelings, confused, not sure how I feel. Love him, don't trust him, want him, don't want him. Feel like giving up—not sure why. Don't feel like we will be able to get back what we had at one time. I sometimes desire to move on to another man. Experience 1st time love again that is full of trust. It would be a lot easier. It would build my self-esteem too. Although I need to depend on myself and God for that—a person cannot give up a good self-esteem. Suspicion claims your mind. Trust, what is that? You fight to believe what he has to say. You feel he loves you yet you fear this is not enough. How does such a poison get in one's veins and destroy a family. How does a man look himself in the mirror and feel that everything is good! That what he has done and what he is going to do to his family is all right. What type of justification can a man have for destroying his wife and children's lives forever! What has happened to the man that I married? Where was his gentle personality and his sweet disposition?

***

Dear Journal,

I haven't written in several weeks. A lot has happened—things, feelings have changed. There are a lot of topics that I have yet to talk about—thoughts in my mind. Probably one of the toughest parts of all this is how I have responded as a mom. It has been difficult to be a mother through all of this. I have been nervous a lot—I can't seem to relax and enjoy my children. I really want to—I think it has gotten better. My kids have suffered beginning this summer for a couple of months now. I get angry at Michael and Teresa for stealing this precious time from me. I was looking forward to a special summer. Children sense and know when things go wrong. When all of this is on your mind and you are a <u>victim</u> to 2 people's selfishness you lose any self-esteem and respect you may have had for yourself. My kids have had to deal with a mom who wasn't sure of herself in a lot of ways. I hope they will forget all of this—especially Chris—he has caught a lot of hell—my personality up and down—I hope we can talk someday about this (he and I). Andrew has been on the back burner. I am so sorry Drew—you are such a great boy!

***

Dear God,

Lord, I really do want our family to work through this situation. God, my self-esteem is gone. I feel so bad about myself as a woman and as a mother. I continue to fight for my husband and my family. The other woman enjoys watching me hurt! Many times I have caught them together and when I did their faces were so full of pride, not of shock or disgrace. Each time I saw their faces all I could see were two people that were liars, cheaters, and had evil, black hearts. How mean two people could possibly be is unbelievable to me. Michael is following the other woman straight to hell and the things that come out of her mouth are poison. You know I have learned a lot in the past few weeks. I have gone through a lot of stages … deep depression, anger, not being able to trust, opening up, learning to lean on others. Godly people are so great! I do not know what I would have done without our Christian friends and my family that has lifted us up in prayer.

***

Dear God,

I am so sleepy—I am in class 1st hour—amazing how I make it everyday. We are separated now. I know it is for the best. I love Michael but I don't love the man that I am seeing now. He confuses me. He thinks he can do what he wants—see her—come see me later and tell me he loves me. What do I do God, hold on or move on! I love my family and do not want to lose it. My son Chris is struggling, what do I do? I love him. I am angry. Michael has walked out on his family and doesn't want the responsibility. The children do not care about him. I hope he is suffering—if he is I sure do not see it. He acts so happy as if nothing has changed. I know God will deal with Michael but what do I do in the meantime. I am so lonely and confused. God where are you! Are you there? Please hold me and my kids close—Lord if it is your will please help my family get back together—if you do not want us with him please let me know. It is hard to see your husband of so many years change so drastically. He has become so selfish not having anything to do with our family. I do not know how to act—loving—firm— standoffish. Please Lord do not let me be bitter—I do not want to be angry or I will never be able to get over all of this. I want to move on with my life and try to build with my kids but I am on hold again for Michael to make up his mind. What do I do God, rush or slow down? I love Michael and I would like to see him come home a healthy person. God please heal his heart. Show Michael things he has not seen before. Please let Teresa show her true colors—I pray that she will let Michael go and lose interest in him. Only a miracle will help us right now. What do I do for the kids! Stay and be patient or let him go! I do not know—God please help me.

***

Dear God,

God where is he? Poisoned by a woman who does not know what love is . . . she only wants to break up our family!! Where is my spiritual leader? Where is the godly man that I married? He needs God more now than ever yet he runs by himself to a dead end. My soul and heart hurt. They yearn for the truth and for an innocent love. We used to have this kind of love. He wants to make excuses for his affair. He seems to want to run from his responsibility as the father and the leader of our family. I believe that if Michael cared about restoring our relationship he would be on his knees every night with me thanking God for our family. He does not play with the children *anymore. He is trying to distance himself so that when he leaves it might be a little easier. My son Christopher is struggling so much. He comes in everyday from school and asks me, "How is daddy doing today?" Constantly he asks me if his dad will be around. Michael bought Chris a shirt from Seattle when he was there visiting during Thanksgiving. There was a lot of turmoil in our home at this time. I told Michael after he came back from Seattle that evening to leave because he had once again stepped out of the marriage. Chris was devastated. Chris got a pair of scissors and cut up the shirt that Michael had given him. Chris felt so guilty about cutting up the shirt. He cried for hours. I held him until he finally fell asleep. Andrew is hitting the other children at school. He has become very aggressive. He told his teacher that his Mom and Dad were fighting. God, hold Andrew's soul in your hands and help him develop into a loving and kind young man.*

***

Dear Journal,

I am still very hurt about last week! It was about this time my husband called me a liar and denied his own son. I wonder how he felt when he saw her again after not seeing her for a while. I hate her—she is just a whore . . . so selfish—I really <u>wish</u> I <u>would hurt her!</u> Physically I wish I could hurt her—I would hit her with my fist or with something else. I am amazed how angry I really am. Coming back to Atlanta—I hate coming back—it only represents bad things. A lot of bad memories. Places we want to go—music—so many things are spoiled. I don't know—wish we could move away. I feel very lonely up here . . . there must be 9 million red convertible cars on the road now and I hate anyone that is blonde and 27 years old. Didn't he know that this would all be so devastating to me and our family? God, I know you are there but please take away the pain and give me the ability to trust my husband.

***

Dear God,

Today I have mixed feelings. I am excited but I am scared. I enjoy having Michael back in our life but I am so afraid that we are going to repeat what has happened. I do not trust him. What I have learned about him scares me—will I ever be able to trust him again? Does he love me like he should—should I have him leave tonight? We have already stayed together for 5 days! I do not know if this has been good or bad. I feel that he does not appreciate totally our family—what I and the children are all about. God please show me what I need to know about Michael—please help him to be strong. I pray for wisdom and discernment, please God, to make wise decisions for myself and my kids. God I want everything to turn out good but I am cautiously excited. Please do not break my heart Michael. I know that I cannot bear the pain anymore. I have given you my heart again and if something happens I know what I will have to do if you fall back into this cycle. Please Lord tell me what to do—Guide me, Oh God.

***

Dear God,

    Interesting weekend—quiet Friday night—Saturday was a different story. Michael came over to play with Chris and Andrew—they had a great day. We all went to Chris's game and then came home and had dinner. We had a great time. Michael and I got into an interesting discussion and a lot was revealed that night. There was an addiction going on I knew about but knew Michael needed to realize this so he would seek help. We have come a long way in a short period of time. I am scared of moving too fast—I am not sure what I want to do—I need more time alone. I need to sort things out.

<u>What I need</u>

1. <u>Space</u>—I have been emotionally scarred for life. I am scared about this happening again. Give me more time alone!

2. I can't have sex with you for a while. I enjoy it but I think of you with the other. I feel it is best for me to not give away my heart so soon!

3. _Accountability_ with a partner and with me about where you are and what you have been doing.

4. Job needs to improve—setting goals.

5. Around the house responsibilities, getting things ready to sell.

6. Actions will speak louder than words.

***

Dear God,

I have been confronted with a lot of new decisions. My husband is a sex addict. Do you understand what this means? At 1st I did not but I will tell you I am reading a lot about it and I am trying to take everything in as slowly as possible. My husband has been into pornography—movies etc. for 25–30 years. The entire time I have been married to him he has been involved with this other life—hidden life. A different man. I wondered why we could not be intimate—lots of times I thought it was me—but I have come to realize that it wasn't me all of the time. I know Michael is frustrated. I can tell. It is a disease of the mind. You can't tell what they are thinking about—I feel so lonely and also like I am sharing my husband's heart (which _is_ your mind) with hundreds of other women! He is not fully mine. His heart is other places. I have never had his heart and I guess his mind. He says he "Loves Me." I really believe he does, it is hard to remember—when you know he is seeing other images or movies and pictures of other women. My biggest question is can I share him for the rest of my life because that is what I will be doing. Will he progressively get worse and worse—it scares me—I feel good about myself—but it is hard to feel really good and complete as a wife and lover. I feel I am sharing my sex life. I have really come into my own on sexuality and I want to have a complete relationship with my husband. Maybe now that it is out in the open, maybe we actually can become much closer. All of the lies and wedges that were between us are out and maybe we can do better. I love my husband and God you are in control—please guide me, Michael and my family to where you want us to be.

***

Michael,

I sit writing this note with a great deal of turmoil in my heart. I see you are hurting and I want to take away that hurt—but I know I can't. You must deal with all of your problems yourself. I am dealing with a few issues myself—one being to "Let Go and Let God" work with you and me—to prepare us for the good and bad times. I guess I try to control more than I think I do. Reason being is because I am scared of being <u>hurt again</u>. I have seen 1st hand how painful this addiction is and it scares me to death. I will tell you it is not Teresa that I am scared of, it is the addiction and what and who it makes you become. I know that without proper treatment and help <u>you</u> will not <u>make</u> it!! We will not make it!

CHAPTER

6

HITTING
BOTTOM

In her last journal entry, Patty expressed concern in a letter written to me that without proper treatment and help, I would not make it. That we would not make it as a family. Her counsel would prove to be prophetic. We separated for good in January of 1998. In November of that year, Patty and I got a divorce. After fifteen years, our marriage was over and our family was torn apart. But it wasn't just over an affair that I wasn't willing to end.

About a year earlier, six months into the affair, I received an unexpected phone call from a close friend, a guy I'd known for most of my life and who knew me pretty well. He wasted no time getting right to the point.

"There's something I need to tell you. I have a sexual addiction."

I was dumbfounded. I didn't know what to say next. What's a sexual addiction? Sounded kind of nasty, like having an STD or contracting AIDS or something. That's not the kind of stuff you go around telling people. I felt a little embarrassed for him.

"Okay, so what's that and why are you telling me this?"

"Well, I'm a sex addict, and I'm telling you because after watching you these past couple of months and hearing you talk about how Patty's not enough and how she doesn't meet your need for intimacy, I'm thinking that you're probably a sex addict too."

I couldn't believe what I was hearing. The audacity of him to even suggest such a thing! I was angry but tried to keep my cool.

"Well, I appreciate you looking out for me, but I'm not so sure I'd agree with you."

I was thinking to myself, *Sorry pal, your problems aren't my problems.* I thought my response put him in his place. But I never expected him to say what he said next.

"Yeah, well, let me tell you a little bit about my past, the stuff I used to do while growing up." He kept on talking, starting with when he was first exposed to pornography as a preteen. He shared details about when he started masturbating to porn, then to scenes of real women undressing in neighborhood homes, and how he used to sneak around and peek into their windows.

I started to feel the sweat making my hands clammy, my pulse starting to quicken. The descriptions of his sexual acting-out behaviors almost paralleled mine. The feelings he would feel and the pain he was trying to run from—it was all too familiar, and definitely more than just a kid occasionally looking at porn. He talked of a relationship he had with the material, his pursuit of the Great Escape, almost as if he had walked by my side every day of my life. I was stunned. I thought I was the only one who did stuff like that. I was busted. Right away, within a matter of minutes of him sharing his story with me, I knew that he knew. And I also knew that he was right.

Our pathological relationships with sex and porn and masturbation were too similar to one another for me to just dismiss it without further investigation. So I set out to do just that. I picked up books on the subject and started reading them. I did some research on the Internet, accessed some sex addiction Web sites, took their online tests, and talked with my friend some more. As I began to think back on my life and all of the secret-world stuff that I did that was related to sex, there was no doubt in my mind that I had a problem. And like most people who finally are able to put a name or attach a label to some kind of behavior and twisted belief system that they could never really explain before, I wanted to run and tell the first person who came to mind—my wife, Patty.

There's nothing like breaking the news to your wife that you've got a sexual addiction, especially just months after confessing that you're having an affair. But that's exactly what happened. And while her journal entries show that at first she had a major struggle trying to get her arms around what exactly that meant for me and for us as a couple, I was amazed at how willing she was to face down this disease of the heart and fight—far more willing, as it turned out, than I was.

In the coming weeks and months, we would go to counseling and attend recovery group meetings, I with other addicts and she with the spouses. We shared reading material, talked about our breakthroughs and setbacks. At times, it was very empowering and brought us much closer together. Finally, it appeared that there might be some light at the end of the tunnel after all. Like our marriage was moving from life support to intensive care. There was hope once again, hope not just of my getting better, but of us coming out of this with a stronger marriage than ever. True intimacy. Trust. A deeper commitment to each other and to our family.

There was only one problem. I didn't want to get well. Not really. I wasn't ready to walk away from either Teresa or the real source of my infidelity, the thousands of women I spent time with every month over the Internet. Women who were mere images, who offered me nothing, but promised me everything. Women I just couldn't say no to, just like I could never really say no to Teresa. I was just as much at her mercy as I was at the mercy of the next image, the coming click of the mouse. That thing over there, on the other side of the fence that I couldn't seem to jump off of. I had my feet firmly planted on both sides, in both worlds, and I wasn't willing to bid either one good-bye. I was straddling a barbed-wire fence, and while I was using porn and sex to numb the pain, it was tearing into every real relationship I had and making a bloody mess out of everything. So I did what I trained myself to do for the better part of my life. I lied. I lied to the counselors. I lied to Patty. I lied to Teresa. I lied to my family and my parents and my friends and to myself. I fabricated stories and emotions and commitments to suit whomever I was trying to pacify, which was usually whoever had the most pain at the moment and was complaining the loudest.

Of course, my lies eventually caught up with me. After a year of seeing me feign my recovery, Patty and the boys lost all hope of my ever getting better. And for a year following our divorce, I continued to fake my way through it—acting remorseful and even breaking down and crying at times in my recovery group meetings and counseling sessions, only to jump right back into my old patterns and acting-out behaviors. The tears and the pronouncements of "never again" weren't all deceptions, but they just weren't true to what my heart was feeling—which was nothing. It was numb. I was numb. I just quit feeling, for others, even for myself. My heart had turned to stone.

It wasn't until a year after our divorce, following my run-in and breakup with Teresa (see introduction) and hearing the news from Patty about her engagement to a guy she had been dating for the past year, that I started to wake up to the realities of what I had done. What I had done. No one else did it to me. I wasn't a helpless victim of some overpowering disease. My circumstances weren't Patty's fault or my parents' fault or society's fault. I made some really selfish, poorly thought-out choices, and now I was beginning to reap the consequences of those choices. The truth was I didn't know what the truth was—about me and who I really was anymore. I had become someone else, someone that even I didn't recognize anymore. When I looked out and saw what a lie Teresa's life was, it was like I was looking into a mirror. But this time, I was starting to see what was really there, lying underneath the polished exterior that I had so painstakingly crafted over the years.

Initially, I felt vindicated when I learned the truth about Teresa and started putting all of the pieces of her sordid existence together. I didn't feel sorry for her, I felt angry. Like she purposefully set out to ruin my life. But upon closer examination, I came to realize that my behaviors, my choices, and my actions were no less harmful to Patty and the boys than Teresa's were to me—and in fact much more so. And I certainly had no intentions when I set out on this journey called life to one day get married and have a family just so I could turn around fifteen years later and destroy their lives. Something had gone terribly wrong, something inside of me that caused me to lose my way. And now, finally, I started paying attention to the signs all around me that were telling me just how lost I was.

It was a terrifying feeling hitting bottom and seeing myself for who I really was. I never felt more alone at any time in my life than I did then. The colors and textures of life changed before my very eyes. The browns and blacks and grays started to dominate my vision. Edges blurred, bright colors faded, sounds became muffled. My mind and my body and my sense of time and space slowed to a crawl and closed in on me. Depression no longer seemed a foreign concept. It became a descriptor of the day-to-day struggle I faced just trying to stay alive, to accomplish basic tasks, to find the slightest bit of joy or happiness or hope in life itself.

Every day I awoke to an ever-expanding sense of guilt and shame over what I had done. Remorse didn't take away the pain; it only made it more vivid in my mind and more agonizing to my heart. Even simple tasks like talking to my boys over the phone took tremendous effort. Picking up the boys every other weekend became emotionally draining as I would often cry for hours before getting them and after returning them to their mom. I didn't just hit bottom and bounce back. I hit bottom and sat there for months on end, for what felt like an eternity.

The lowest depth of the bottom finally came for me one night while lying prostrate on the floor in my apartment. I had just finished going for my customary long walk at night. The apartment complex where I lived was located in a large suburban Atlanta office and shopping district. It was a far cry from the neighborhood pool and ballparks of west Cobb County where I had spent so much of my time with my family.

As I walked the back streets of these massive office complexes at night, I would often talk to myself or talk to God and just cry out for mercy. I didn't know what else to do. I was too depressed after coming home from work to go out at night. Most of my friends had bailed on me. And I didn't blame them. All I had was my job and my two boys every other weekend. On this night, I was in an especially dark mood. The last few nights out had been a real struggle. I was beating myself up pretty good. And it was all I could do to come in the door afterwards and just collapse on the floor. Tonight, like the last few nights, a faint voice inside of me was again suggesting a way out. A way to escape the pain I was feeling, but this time for good.

"It can all go away, you know. The pain. It can be gone once and for all. Forever."

I so wanted the pain to go away. My Great Escape was only compounding my hurt and consequences and making me feel worse instead of taking the pain away, as it always had before. I still turned to it, but by now I knew that it wasn't the solution; it was part of the problem. So now I was trying to go as long as I could without resorting to porn, white-knuckling it, as they say. And after only a few days without, I was really hurting. It was like I was going through some kind of drug withdrawal. I felt defenseless against the onrush of these emotions without it. The pain inside was now far greater than anything I had ever felt or imagined before.

The voice continued, "You know you've blown it. You're forty years old. You'll never get these years back with your kids. Patty's moved on, found true love. You lied to her. She'll never forgive you. She doesn't love you anymore. The boys don't love you anymore. Nobody wants you anymore." It was relentless. And then came the Offer.

"But you can make the pain go away once and for all. All you have to do is just walk next door to the Wal-Mart and buy a gun. You know they sell guns there. Then, just put the barrel in your mouth and pull the trigger and you'll never have to feel this pain again."

I seriously considered the Offer. It was tempting. I started thinking through the details of how I'd do it. I decided that I'd buy a revolver instead of a shotgun. *Less messy*, I figured. I also decided that I wouldn't do it in the den. *Carpet stains would be too much trouble for someone to clean up afterwards. The kitchen, with its linoleum floors, would be much better.* I'm not sure why I became so concerned about how clean or messy the crime scene would be. But I was starting to think through the particulars of how I was going to kill myself. I was tired and I just wanted the pain to go away.

The next step would be writing a suicide note.

Let's see, what to say to my boys . . . Tears started filling my eyes. I began trembling with fear. And then I stopped. *No! I'm not doing it! I'm NOT going to leave THAT kind of legacy behind for my boys!* Before I knew it I had picked myself up off the floor and was brushing my pants off and wiping my tears away.

I choose life. At that moment, in a way I still grasp for the right words to describe, I felt a presence, the presence of God with me. I realize that sounds weird to a lot of people. But it's like He was there with me the whole time. I started thinking about that. And the more I thought about it, the more I realized that God had been with me for a long time. I just hadn't been present for God. I thought it was like when you're hanging out with someone, but you might as well be alone because they're so preoccupied with something else. Or someone else. Then I thought, *I wonder if that's how Patty and the boys felt around me these past few years. I was with them, but I wasn't really with them.*

"I choose life." I said it out loud. I liked the way it sounded. "I'm going to get better. I'm going to get my life back." As I made my way back to the bedroom, I fell on top of the covers with my clothes still on and fell fast asleep. I was exhausted, and there was much to do tomorrow. It was time to start getting well.

CHAPTER

7

GETTING WELL

It took losing a fifteen-year marriage, my boys, my job, my friends, my reputation, my affair partner, any hopes of reconciling with and remarrying Patty, and a whole lot of money before I finally hit bottom. That's what it took to finally get my attention.

I'm thankful that it didn't take more—AIDS, an unwanted pregnancy, a doomed marriage to Teresa, or a suicide—mine, Patty's, or perhaps one of the boys'. But that's often what happens in the insane world of addiction. The unthinkable becomes reality as reality becomes an accumulation of consequence after consequence. There would still be a big price to pay for how far I did go, both in my life and in the lives of so many others. But all of that had yet to play itself out.

Hitting bottom for me wasn't one isolated event, although my brush with suicide certainly marked a turning point. It was more like walking along the bottom of a long, dark tunnel. When I did wake up, it literally felt like stepping out of the tunnel's darkness and into the light of day. I could see things much more clearly now. I could also feel hope rising again. And why not? I mean, how much worse could it get? Feeling like the worst could be behind me was a big motivator in choosing to get well. So I set out to do just that. Fortunately, I had a pretty decent job working in sales for a local software firm. This one I was able to keep. The job offered me stability, constancy, and the opportunity to build my self-esteem back. But other than that, I was totally lost. The good news was I knew it. I knew I needed help.

The first thing I did was start going to church again. On the surface that might not sound like a very big deal. But for me, it was. Growing up as a kid, going to church on Sunday was something my dad made me do. He made all of us go to church, telling us that it would help us be better kids or something like that. I'm sure that's the same reason they sent us to private Christian schools for eight years.

The older I got, the more I rebelled against going to church. I used to go to services later in the day than my parents, so my dad would drop me off and then plan to swing back by afterwards to pick me up. I'd step inside the door, grab a church bulletin, wait for a few minutes for him to drive off, then exit through a side door and head straight to the grocery store across the street to look at magazines. As services were about to end, I'd walk back to the church and hang around outside waiting for him to pick me up, church bulletin in hand. The con seemed to work, but I'm sure he figured out what I was doing after a while. I think by then there was only so much fight left in him, and this just wasn't something worth fighting over.

I didn't really have anything against God, or so I thought. My bone to pick was with my dad. I was convinced that his reasons for why we had to go to church were lame—the most often heard were "because I said so" and "because I'm your father." That used to work when I was younger, but not as a teen. Eventually, I quit going to church altogether when I went off to college. Oh, I'd go to church with my family during the holidays, but it was mostly to pacify my dad. I'm not even sure how much my mom really wanted to be there since she grew up Protestant and only converted to Catholicism after meeting and planning to marry my dad. As for me, I didn't get it. All those years growing up and attending Catholic schools, going to Mass, and being an altar boy, and at the end of the day, it still felt like my parents' religion.

But after years of having a critical and judgmental attitude toward my dad and the church, and when I finally reached a point in my life where I realized I didn't have all the answers, my mind would replay the countless times I remembered walking into my parents' bedroom and seeing this giant of a man down on his knees next to my mom with his head poured into his hands as he prayed to God. Looking back, I wish my dad and I would have had more conversations about God. I would have loved knowing what he prayed about, what he thought about when he thought about God, and why it was so important to him to go to church, though I'm not sure I would have really listened back then. But my dad's faith in God was mostly a personal and private thing. I think he must have thought that the church and those nuns and priests that ran our school were in a better position and could do a better job of explaining all of that to us. And God knows they tried. But there were a lot of things I didn't understand about God and my father's beliefs that required some additional explanation. It was the same way with sex and trying to understand what I was going through during puberty. Or what to do when I felt the urge to masturbate. Or how to handle a situation when a girl I was with wanted to have sex with me. It would have been nice to have been able to talk with my mom or my dad about that kind of stuff. But especially my dad.

Going back to church was the single most significant thing I did during my recovery. It was my way of saying, "You're God, and I'm not!" That was important for me to acknowledge because I'd been acting and treating other people like I was God for years.

I also started opening the Bible and reading it again, like I had done at different times throughout my marriage. Only this time, it wasn't for show. There was no one to impress, no one to convince that I was religious and righteous and all. I just started reading the Gospels—the books of Matthew, Mark, Luke, and John—and found myself learning more about who Jesus was than I did in all of my years of parochial school combined.

I would get excited when I read verses that said that Jesus came not to judge the world but to save sinners like me. I also liked it when I read about Jesus' humanity, and how He suffered and was faced with the same temptations that we face every day. But most of all, I hungered for truth. I was starving to read and hear the truth about who God was and who He said I was. The pastor at the church I attended used the Bible a lot in his preaching, and I hung on every word and every verse and every explanation. It gave me a starting point and something to measure the health of my recovery and relationships by.

I also started praying again. I'll never forget one of my first prayers after nearly taking my own life. It was, "God, please show me how to talk to You again. And how to listen." That's it. That was all I could get out in the midst of my guilt and shame. It was simply the first honest thought that I had. Since that day, I don't ever remember my prayers, my conversations with God, being so relaxed and feeling so natural before. I was tired of faking it, tired of years of pretense and posing. It was time to get real with God.

I also started seeing a counselor again. He was a Christian counselor who had a lot of experience dealing with sex addicts. That was very important to me because I knew how cunning I could be. We addicts were world-class, pathological liars. I think it helped that he was a recovering sex addict too. I knew that probably meant he knew most if not all of my tricks, my smoke screens, and my justifications and rationalizations.

Right away he invited me to attend his Monday night faith-based therapy group. The time I spent in recovery groups was incredibly helpful, especially during the early stages of recovery. I went to other 12-step groups, too, that didn't talk much about spiritual things. It didn't matter to me at the time, I just knew I needed help. And there was something powerful and life changing in knowing that you weren't the only one facing these kinds of struggles. It starts to take the power away from the addiction and gives you room to breathe again.

The other element of recovery groups that made a huge difference in my life came when it was my turn to share about my struggles. When I confessed the stuff I was doing, most of which I had never shared with anyone before, it was a relief to look around the room and notice that no one was bolting for the doors or saying, "Wow, dude, you've got some serious problems. How could you do something like that?" Instead, I read the facial expressions of those around me and could see understanding and mercy and grace and sorrow. Then someone offered, "Yeah, I know what that feels like," or "Wow, I thought I was the only one who did that." Nothing that I've ever done has had a greater impact in restoring hope in my life than the time I've spent in recovery groups. Nor have I since experienced a greater sense of honesty and authenticity and kinship with a group of people.

I ended up attending those weekly sessions for several years, then intermittently for a year or two after that. I had been involved in recovery groups before, but that was when I was feigning my recovery while still acting out. My main motivation in going to meetings back then was to keep Patty and my counselors off my back. I never really wanted to get well.

When I entered recovery the second time, I really worked hard on my stuff, on truth-telling, trying to understand my family-of-origin issues, and working to stay sober, which by our group's definition meant abstaining from sex with self (masturbation) or others outside of marriage. I recruited several accountability partners, guys I could call any time of the day or night who I knew would listen and could help me stay sober. And after experimenting with different Internet site blockers and filters, I finally settled on a piece of accountability software from a company called Covenant Eyes that would send weekly reports of Web sites that I visited to my accountability partners, flagging those sites that might contain objectionable material. I found this to be the greatest technology-based tool for recovery, and it's still something I rely on to this day.

There is much more to say about getting well than the space in this chapter could possibly allow, and it is a topic that I'll be revisiting in later chapters. But two guiding principles or truths have underscored my own success in recovery for the past ten years.

The first, what I refer to as Recovery or Healing for the Whole Person, is understanding that recovery is a healing process that involves both physiological and spiritual healing. The second is an operating principle or law that drives the first, much like an operating system drives the functioning of a computer. I call it The Law of Increase/Decrease, and it simply says that "what you feed grows, and what you starve dies." Once you understand the workings of these two guiding principles in your own recovery or even other areas of your life, you'll be able to not only measure your progress but also predict your outcome. It's really quite simple.

First, Healing for the Whole Person. I spent a lot of time in and was helped considerably by sexual addiction recovery groups, which for the most part operate very much like AA (Alcoholics Anonymous), OA (Overeaters Anonymous), GA (Gamblers Anonymous)—essentially all of the "As," as I call them. Just in the area of sexual addiction recovery alone, there's SA (Sexaholics Anonymous), SAA (Sex Addicts Anonymous), and SLAA (Sex and Love Addicts Anonymous).

While it's true that AA, the pioneers of the 12-step addiction recovery process, had spiritual roots and actually integrated both physiological behavior modification and a simplified version of cognitive therapy with spiritual awakening and renewal processes, many "As" operating today have sadly evolved into a model that emphasizes physiological healing and minimizes or downplays spiritual healing. That was never the original intention or design of the architects of an integrated process of healing that has literally saved the lives and livelihoods of millions of people.

What one sometimes experiences today when engaging this postmodern model are people who have become prisoners of a strictly physiological form of behavior modification. I have personally met many men and women who have been "set free" from their addiction to sex or alcohol or drugs, only to become addicted to recovery. They're junkies of the process of recovery who are being duped out of experiencing the intended product of recovery: true healing and freedom from addiction. It's kind of like baking a cake but only using half of the ingredients called for in the recipe. You may end up with something you choose to call a cake, but it's not going to taste anything like the real thing. Healing for the Whole Person uses all of the ingredients, and while the desired outcome is never guaranteed (after all, the cook and his motivation are big variables), it is much more likely.

Of course, the same thing can happen in reverse, and I've seen it all too often, especially in the church. A faith-based recovery group gets started in a church and decides to put an emphasis on spiritual healing and deliverance. Believing that faith in God and prayer alone can move mountains and heal any addict (which it can if God so chooses), they downplay or outright ignore the significance of physiological healing. More often than not they end up with frustrated group members who feel more guilty and shameful than ever and don't understand why God didn't answer their prayers and take their sexual addiction away.

What they didn't stop to realize is that in the spiritual healing process, just like the spiritual growth process, typically there's God's part and there's man's part. For instance, my part in dealing with the physiological process of healing may require that I give up using the Internet or watching cable TV for a period of time to simply help my mind and my body go through a detoxification and cleansing process. Praying, "God, cleanse my mind of all impure thoughts and take away the temptation to commit sexual sin," then sitting down to watch an episode of *Sex and the City* is just another form of a cake baked with half the ingredients. The process of healing must address the pathology that exists in both the physiological and the spiritual realm if there is going to be healing for the whole person.

Regulating that healing process is our second guiding principle, the Law of Increase/Decrease. Simply stated, it says that what you feed grows, and what you starve dies. Interestingly enough, this same principle is at work in the escalation and establishment of the addiction to begin with. For instance, as a sex addict feeds his lustful desires what they long for—sexual images, thoughts, fantasies, and experiences—his sexual compulsivity grows. Feed your sexual impulses with sexual experiences, and your sexual impulsiveness and acting-out behaviors increase.

As Newton's Third Law of Motion has shown us, for every action, there is an equal and opposite reaction. In the same way, the Decrease part of the law also kicks in automatically. For example, when you're busy feeding one thing, you're necessarily starving another. In this case, as you're feeding lust and watching it grow, you're also starving love and watching it die. Feed fantasy relationships, and your fantasy world grows. But in the process, you are starving real relationships, and they will begin to die. Feed yourself a steady diet of pornography, and you'll increasingly view women as degraded sex objects—you'll sexualize and objectify all women. And in the process of doing that, you'll have fewer and fewer thoughts and images representing a healthy view of women as caring, loving, feeling individuals worthy of your admiration and respect. As you starve your mind of those healthy images of women, the idea or concept of women being anything but sex objects continues to die and fade away.

Now, considering the fact that the average American consumer is exposed to over 14,000 sexual images and messages every year,[1] most of which objectify women and base their value on their body shape and size, you can see where the Law of Increase/Decrease plays a major role in both addiction and recovery. Once I understood the basics of how this law worked, it became an effective tool for recovery that I used every day, and still do.

Whenever I identified a certain aspect of my addiction that I was feeding, or something healthy that I was starving, I'd "flip" it in my mind and apply the opposite part of the equation. For instance, instead of "feeding" myself sexual images from cable TV or the Internet, I'd "starve" myself of them. And if I found that I was "starving" myself of healthy relationships by isolating, I would look for opportunities to "feed" myself by getting more socially involved. Of course, as I did that, the Law of Increase/Decrease guaranteed the outcome. By feeding myself healthy relationships and growing my circle of friends, I was starving my feelings of loneliness and isolation and killing my insecurities and feelings of insignificance.

The constant awareness of these two powerful principles at work has given me sustainability and success throughout my recovery from sexual addiction, an affliction that typically reports low success rates of long-term sobriety. And as I continue to work out my own issues, it's only by God's grace and mercy that my recovery can become much more than just the absence of unwanted sexual behaviors. Nearly ten years into the process, I've been able to move past focusing most of my time and attention on stopping the "bottom line" sexual acting-out behaviors and put more time and energy into developing healthy relational intimacy. After many years of struggling through dating relationships with various intimacy issues as a "love disabled" person, I'm finishing the writing of this book while standing on the precipice of marriage once again. And instead of being terrified, I'm confident and ready to be the loving, caring partner my bride-to-be, Christine, has always hoped for in a husband.

Today, my recovery continues on as it will throughout the rest of my life. But it has become about more than just the reconciliation and restoration of broken relationships, the healing of life-long wounds, and the conveyance of a message of hope to a hurting world that longs for a solution. It's about discovering real life and true intimacy amidst the reality of painful emotions and broken dreams. It's about feeling again so you can be alive to all that life has to offer, and learning to face the truth about yourself and others, not just for the sake of being fully known and loved, but so that you can know what it feels like to fully know and love others well. For in recovery, as in the rest of life, The Truth about Me is really just a microcosm of the greater Truth about Us.

PART 2

THE TRUTH ABOUT US

CHAPTER

8

A
PERFECT
STORM

A *perfect storm* refers to the simultaneous occurrence of events which, taken individually, would be far less powerful than the result of their chance combination.

Thinking back on how the events of my life have unfolded leading up to my recovery, it certainly felt like I was being tossed about and pressed upon by several converging storm fronts—the ever-changing economic and societal trends that make up our current culture. These "fronts" are the atmospheric dynamics that form the setting for each of our stories. Becoming aware of them allowed me to develop a strategy for avoiding potential landmines and falling back into the dark chasm of addiction.

Addictions are unwanted habitual behaviors and dependencies, usually based on a set of false beliefs we hold about ourselves, others, and the world we live in. You can never hope to overcome addiction or change bad habits if you fail to understand the context in which they flourish.

So this part of the book is all about context. But before we jump into how you can guard yourself against a potential fall (or for those already down and fighting their way back, how to recover), we're going to uncover, examine, and expose what's really going on here from a higher vantage point. The only disclaimer I'd like to offer is to remind the reader that my intentions here are not to provide an exhaustive, objective, and unbiased perspective on these broad topics, each of which has been dissected and written about extensively. On the contrary, my goal is to provide a very biased, highly opinionated commentary on each based on my own personal experience, giving my readers insight into what the world looks like through the lens of a recovering sex addict. Hopefully, you'll find value in receiving that perspective, much the way a person in charge of bank security benefits from the wise counsel of a reformed career bank robber.

With that said, I'll begin by taking a closer look at the three major individual storm fronts that I see converging over our culture today. I believe that their simultaneous occurrence and growing interdependence are giving birth to a perfect storm that will rain down social and personal consequences unlike any great society has witnessed before.

STORM FRONT #1 - HYPERSEXUAL MEDIA

There's an old advertising industry saying that's been around forever—Sex Sells! I remember first hearing that phrase back in the late '70s when I was taking a Mass Media business course in college. This was about ten years after the so-called sexual revolution took root in our country. As we searched through liquor and cigarette company print ads looking for cunningly disguised phallic symbols or the form of a woman's body hidden in a glass of ice, it dawned on me that while this might be a fun way to spend our time in class, it seemed pretty irrelevant to the overall scheme of life. I mean, if I wanted to see a woman's legs or breasts

I knew just where to find them. And it wasn't on TV or in grocery store magazine racks.

A lot has changed in a few decades. Radio, print, broadcast, and now new media have always been aware of the competitive advantage they had in using any and all things sexual as a way to get and keep their audiences' attention. But never before have they enjoyed operating in a climate of such permissive sexual values and mores. The result has been an unprecedented rise in both the use and acceptance of increasingly pornographic depictions of sex in all forms of mainstream media.

For example, one popular study on the amount of sexual content on basic cable and network television found that the number of sex scenes nearly doubled between 1998 and 2005.[1] The study found that 70% of all shows, excluding daily newscasts, sports events, and children's shows, include some sexual content, averaging five sex scenes per hour. Yet out of those shows with sexual content, only 14% included at least one scene with a reference to sexual risks or responsibilities. In other words, they used sex to sell.

While literally thousands of studies conducted since the 1950s have proven a link between exposure to media violence and violent behavior,[2] relatively little attention has been paid to the impact that exposure to a rising tide of sexual content (14,000 sexual images and messages each year on television alone[3]) is having on the average American consumer. One recent study on teens found that watching sex on television increases the chances a teen will have sex, and may cause teens to start having sex at younger ages.[4] But other than a few studies scattered here and there, attended by a lot of rhetoric claiming everything from no harm done to predictors of sexual criminality, most of what we know about the impact of our sex-saturated mainstream media on real people and relationships is anecdotal.

What I do know as a recovering sex addict is that TV and the portrayal of sex in the media have been and always will be key potential triggers for me that could lead to unwanted sexual behaviors. The growing prevalence of sexual images, innuendo, and sexualized objectification even on basic cable is a constant threat to my sexual sobriety. Song lyrics, music videos, reality TV shows, sitcoms, commercials, print ads, and even the covers of magazines at my local supermarket checkout dot the landscape of my life like land mines waiting to explode under my feet should I choose to ponder them for too long.

But even as I talk with today's youth and college students, the real target of this growing industry with an insatiable appetite for profits comes as no surprise to them. The most common response I get when asking them if they're aware of their exposure to all of the titillating content around them: "Sure, we know, we're soaking in it!" When asked how it's affecting them, most can only shrug their shoulders. Like the proverbial frog enjoying a swim in the boiling pot sitting on a stove, all we really know is it's a good bit warmer in here than it used to be.

STORM FRONT #2 - ENABLING TECHNOLOGIES

If our hypersexual media is busy painting us a picture of a world that is increasingly pornographic, then it's through the application and availability of enabling technologies that we now have access to this wide world of adult entertainment anytime, anywhere, and in practically any form or medium we choose. Since long before the advent of film and photography, creating images of people as sexual beings has always fascinated us. Yet until recently it's been a niche market and industry unto itself with significant barriers to reaching consumers, severe legal restraints, and an unseemly cast of characters content with living life on the lowest rungs of society and industry.

But with a few key technology decisions made along the way, perhaps the most notable being the shift from expensive film production and theater distribution to emerging VHS video technologies, the marriage between porn and technology was consummated. It was a bold move that gave the porn industry access to the masses and their millions of home VCRs. As they became rich and continued to grow, they could afford to invest heavily in technology, pioneering or perfecting such breakthroughs as CD-ROMs, streaming video, and online payment systems. Fast-forward to today's digital world where new media content creation technologies and distribution processes are constantly reinventing themselves (think YouTube), and you have an environment ripe for "technology of the masses, by the masses, and for the masses." New markets are being created by consumers, not companies. Suddenly, as in so many other business sectors trying to stay ahead of the technological game, adult entertainment industry executives frequently find themselves on the outside looking in.

Today's technology consumers now have the ability to create their own porn. They can shoot it, act in it, brand it, package it, market it, and distribute it locally, regionally, or globally. All without the help or knowledge of the porn industry itself. The Internet, consumer electronics, and a host of other digital computer and communication technologies have made all of this possible. That and an independent consumer who is less willing to settle for prepackaged porn.

I had a front-row seat in this evolutionary process while spending over two decades working in the technology industry for companies like IBM, NEC, Unisys, and many others. I was also an avid consumer and early adopter of technology-driven porn throughout that time. But nothing compared to the exponential leap that the development of the Internet represented in terms of the increased accessibility, affordability, and anonymity that one could enjoy while consuming the material. The commodification of high-speed Internet access that followed was like adding gasoline to a brush fire. It just took off, for me and about 18 to 22 million others who are now sexually addicted. This unique combination of attributes (accessibility, affordability, and anonymity), commonly referred to as the "Triple-A Engine"[5] of Internet porn, lends itself particularly well to the development of sexually compulsive and addictive behaviors since together they intensify, accelerate, and allow you to hide online sexual behaviors. Unfortunately, I had to learn this firsthand.

To be sure, technology can bring good things to life. But the misuse or misapplication of it, whether by individual consumers or whole industries, only means that some of us will arrive at our unintended destinations much quicker than others. Or to borrow from the pitch phraseology of Madison Avenue: "Why take thirty years like I did when you, too, can have the same sexual addiction in just a few short months?!"

STORM FRONT #3 - SOCIOSEXUAL PATHOLOGIES

In December 2003, Faith Popcorn, one of the most respected marketing trend experts in American business, was asked by the Wall Street Journal to forecast the major trends in business for the coming year (2004). This was her response: "Porn will become the norm. Nothing shocks anyone anymore. Our shock button has been turned off and that is why advertisers are finding it hard to get their messages through. The whole country is desensitized. The media will continue to push the limits of what's acceptable."[6]

In addition to speaking volumes about the state of our hypersexual media, this prediction, which most will agree has come true, should serve as a warning sign to us all that as a society personified, we are a sick patient and getting worse by the minute. Within the life span of a single generation, the things that we once considered unthinkable are now defended as matters of personal choice that demand tolerance, no matter how offensive they may seem. As we move the line of decency into territory representing the more raw and extreme genres of porn, a new norm is forming in our collective societal conscience. We increasingly sexualize what we see, while growing numb to the consequences. Although definitive studies on the effects of porn can be hard to find, there is some work that's been done in this area. Take for instance the landmark studies on students that were held simultaneously at UCLA and St. Xavier College back in the mid-90s. Both men and women were exposed to over four hours of erotic video (of varying types: soft, hardcore, etc.) and then asked to answer a set of questions meant to gauge their attitudes toward sex crimes. All of the men proved to be more accepting of rape myths (that is, that women who are raped "ask for it" or secretly enjoy the experience) and, surprisingly, over half of the women as well.[7] Women in these films were portrayed as insatiable and in need of constant sexual fulfillment, the norm in porn.

The Meese Commission report from the Reagan era bent over backwards to try to show a connection between consumption of pornography and sex crimes, rape, and murder. While sex crimes in general have certainly increased over the past twenty years, the overall doom and gloom predictions were a bit alarmist.

Then there's the other side of the equation. Academicians and sex workers alike will defend their conviction that there isn't nearly enough wide-open sexuality yet to liberate our repressive society. They carry the mantra of people like Alfred Kinsey, Hugh Hefner, and Larry Flynt who saw or see themselves on a mission to set America, but mostly themselves, free sexually. Both camps can be annoying, and if you spend too much time soaking in their ideology, your head will start to spin.

This is why I believe when it comes down to really understanding how far our sociosexual pathology has taken us, you needn't look much further than our own personal experiences, our current attitudes, and the people around us. Think of how your own sexual viewpoints, beliefs, and behaviors have changed in the past ten to twenty years. Parents, look at yourself and your peers, not to mention those younger than you and your own children. Singles and teens, look at yourself and some of the kids you grew up with. Most parents I talk with are shocked when I tell them what many teenagers and college-age kids are into sexually. And yet when I talk with college students and share what junior high and high school students are doing sexually, most of them are shocked too. "What!?! We don't even do that!" is a common response. The lines of decency and sexual integrity have shifted, and old values are constantly replaced by new ones. But at what price? How far can the boundaries be pushed before someone gets hurt?

In the midst of our changing society and the culture wars and ideological firefights that seem to accompany change, a new generation is rising. The first kids to grow up on Internet porn have come of age and are now teenagers. They are the youngest offspring of the baby boomers, the newly minted citizens of our Porn Nation. They're Generation Sex, the so-called Cyberporn Generation. Together with their older siblings they're also becoming the New Pornographers. Armed with the latest tools of technology, they're busy rewriting all the rules and quickly making the business model of the porn industry obsolete. Born out of our culture's Perfect Storm, they're the change agents of a new sexual revolution that will eclipse the old and have a dramatic impact on each and every one of us, for better and for worse. Perhaps now we really *do* have something to worry about.

CHAPTER

9

GENERATION SEX
and the **NEW**
PORNOGRAPHERS

In June of 2004, *People* magazine published a feature article titled "Cyberporn Generation" that grabbed my attention. What captivated me more than the provocative title was what I read in the subtitle: "The first kids to grow up with Internet porn come of age."[1]

Like most parents, and as the father of two boys (the youngest being nine when this article was written), I have been concerned about how to protect our children from accidental exposure to the unhealthy sexual images and messages that proliferate on the Web. But the thought of a generation of kids hitting puberty and becoming active porn consumers really hit me hard. It seems like a lifetime ago when I was eleven years old and getting my first glimpses of naked women. But I know all too well that the material I viewed back then was tame in comparison to what's available today with a quick click of a mouse.

I wondered what my reaction would be if I were a kid growing up today and my first exposure to porn were watching a sex tape online of Paris or Britney or Tommy Lee and Pam, or some other pop culture icon I might have been following on TV. What if it were seeing random pictures of group sex on a porn site? Or a picture of a group of smiling teens appearing naked in an Abercrombie & Fitch clothes catalog with the caption "Group Sex" superimposed below it? What would I think if I watched the president of the United States pronounce to millions of TV viewers that he "did not have sex with that woman," Monica Lewinsky, because as far as he was concerned, oral sex wasn't really sex? How would that make me feel about my own sexuality? What if I had just viewed a video of a teenage girl having sex with a horse, or a dog, or her mom and dad (or so they claimed)? What if the naked pictures or videos I saw weren't on some porn site, but it was on MySpace or YouTube, maybe even involving someone I recognize from my school? How would I define normal if this is where I were learning about sex?

A LOOK AT THE STATISTICS

The scenarios I've portrayed above are not uncommon. In fact, studies show that for today's teens, they're very much the norm. The average age of first exposure to commercial pornography is somewhere between 11 and 14.[2] But with one in four children in nursery school (ages 3, 4, and 5) going online,[3] that average age is sure to drop. In fact, as I've informally surveyed high school and college students myself over the last several years, I've talked to many students who claim they were first exposed to pornography at age 4 or 5.

With studies showing us that over 80% of teens age 15 to 17 have had multiple exposure to hard-core pornography,[4] it's hard to imagine that pornography *wouldn't* play some role in influencing the sexual attitudes, beliefs, and behaviors of this generation just as it has past generations. Even if the exposure is limited to the 14,000 sexual images and messages that appear yearly on television, the influences are still there.

Studies have shown that adolescents who watch television with high levels of sexual content are twice as likely to initiate sexual intercourse and also more likely to initiate other sexual activities.[5] And teens with high levels of exposure to rap videos, which often promote drug use, violence, and sex, are significantly more likely to acquire an STD.[6]

With one-third of teenage guys and one-fourth of teenage girls feeling some or a lot of pressure to have sex,[7] 27% of teens between the ages of 13 and 16 are now sexually active.[8] In fact, over half of teens ages 15–19 say they've had oral sex,[9] and nearly half (42% of guys and 33% of girls ages 15–17) have had intercourse.[10] And while both parents and teens report talking to each other about sex and relationships, there appears to be a disconnect: twice as many parents as teens maintain these conversations happen often (85% to 41%).[11]

As a result, while 27% of teens report having been sexually intimate, only about half of their parents (15%) believed their teens had gone beyond kissing.[12] That leaves their peers and pornographers as their primary sex educators. We can't expect our sex-saturated society to give our kids a healthy view of sex, love, and relationships. Yet that's what many of us as parents and educators are doing, just like our parents did with us.

Lately I've started asking more questions of my own son as he enters puberty and his teenage years—questions about what kind of sexual images he's seen and what his friends look at and what they talk about when they talk about sex. Most of the time, I'm met with pretty much the same kind of response I used to give my parents on those rare occasions when they tried to talk to me about sex. "Huh? Oh, that. Not much. No, we don't look at that stuff." Everything I say to him after that sounds preachy, like I'm talking *at* him instead of with him. Before I know it, we're off discussing safer subjects like the local sports teams or what he's doing at school. Short of those rare, honest exchanges that some of us parents have with our teens about sex, what do we really know about Generation Sex, the Cyberporn Generation?

One thing we know is that they're immersed in a world of technology-driven products, and as a result most are quite comfortable with it because that's all they've known. My oldest son, Chris, reminded me that his suburban high school didn't add Internet capability until just before his junior year in 2002. But for my youngest son, Andrew, all he's ever known whenever he turns on a computer or uses a cell phone is that he has the ability to access any information and communicate instantly with anyone at any time about anything.

So it's not surprising that 96% of kids under the age of 18 have gone online, 74% have access at home, and 61% use the Internet on a typical day.[13] Seventy-three percent of teens report they have a desktop computer, 45% report they have a cell phone, 18% say they have a laptop computer, and 7% have a personal digital device such as a Palm Pilot.[14] Teens today are plugged in and turned on like never before. And as new technologies and technology-based services are introduced, Generation Sex more often than not is identified as early adopters. But just as we've learned with the Internet, having fast access to all the world has to offer doesn't come without its pitfalls.

Take the red-hot wireless market, for example. By the end of 2004, more than 60% of Americans were using wireless devices to talk, send e-mail, take pictures, make and watch videos, and listen to music. In the same year, the number of wireless subscribers in the United States surpassed 180.5 million, with revenue topping $102 billion, up 21.7 million subscribers from 2003, according to CTIA, the wireless trade association.[15] And a growing percentage of wireless users are teens.

A 2004 market research report showed that 40% of 15–19 year olds in the United States are wireless subscribers. The report went on to describe teens as "the classic early adopters" who play "a central role in the early adoption and mass-market acceptance of wireless data capabilities, ranging from short message service (SMS), to gaming, to ring-tones, and are increasingly helping to drive adoption and usage of new applications such as picture and video messaging."[16]

What looms on the horizon is starting to look like a repeat performance of what pornographers were able to do by leveraging Internet and cable TV technologies to their advantage. Only this time, we're talking about putting porn in your pocket. By early 2004, selling sexual content or pornography over cell phones had already started generating considerable profits for wireless companies in Western Europe.[17] The Yankee Group predicts the mobile adult-content business will be worth $1 billion worldwide by 2008, while Juniper Research has it at $2.1 billion by 2009.[18]

By the time you combine the growing use of cell phones by teens and preteens with the increased availability of wireless Internet access and adult content over wireless devices, you've created a world for kids where they can privately and discreetly access high-res pornographic pictures and video from mobile devices at any time and from anywhere. If wireless market trends and forecasts hold true, it could create a nightmare for parents and an epidemic of sexual pathologies.

THE NEW PORNOGRAPHERS

Much of what I've focused on has to do with Generation Sex as an emerging yet increasingly desensitized and overexposed group of porn consumers. But what is even more alarming is the trend toward porn consumers becoming porn producers who create their own content. With the availability of low-cost consumer electronics and access to easy-to-use software and Web-based tools, the customer can now customize content to his heart's desire. And that capability alone poses a significant threat to the commercial porn industry. No longer do they own the domain of adult entertainment. These "New Pornographers," as I call them, are content creators and content distributors who fly under the radar of both regulators and commercial enterprises. Thanks to the surging popularity of social networking sites like MySpace, YouTube, and FaceBook, over 100 million users have learned how to upload and share digital images and video content for a worldwide audience.

Shot with Web cams and cell phones with built-in cameras, this homegrown brand of reality porn is as real as it gets. It comes at a time when the commercial porn industry is scrambling to make up for lost revenue from declining adult video rentals and sales. As the Internet explodes with free access to homemade amateur videos, the contrived productions the commercial porn industry is so famous for just aren't cutting it with savvy porn consumers anymore. Even young, under-age consumers are turning away from the come-ons and the hardened 20- and 30-something actresses dressed in ponytails and cheerleader outfits to look a fraction of their age. Reality or "gonzo" porn, as it's sometimes called, is a hot market on the Internet, with amateurs and uninhibited teens bypassing the industry altogether to share their own sexual images and messages with a growing network of friends and ac-quaintances.

The New Pornographers differ greatly from their old-economy counterparts. Apart from the obvious differences in age and experience (most haven't left their teens or twenties yet and have no prior history working in the adult entertainment industry), the vast majority of New Pornographers aren't motivated by money like those in the commercial porn industry. It usually has more to do with gaining celebrity status within their peer group, acting on a desire and curiosity to explore their sexual identity, or just getting noticed. Such behavior is not necessarily a sign of sexual compulsivity or addiction, although exhibitionism and voyeurism don't exactly set a promising precedent, especially for teens.

Most disturbing to commercial porn producers is the cost-free and easily distributable content. I wouldn't expect to hear porn industry pundits raise their voices over this, but there's no doubt that it's hurting their business.

But that's the furthest thing from the minds of Generation Sex and the New Pornographers. Theirs is a bold new world where they're in control, or so they think. These pioneers of Porn Nation's new economy have the ability to put themselves or their friends in the spotlight even though the set may only be a dimly lit dorm room and the actress may literally be the girl next door.

CHAPTER

10

I AM *NOT* CHARLOTTE SIMMONS

Several years ago renowned American author Tom Wolfe wrote a bestseller entitled *I Am Charlotte Simmons*. The story chronicles the modern-day experiences of college life as seen through the eyes of "beautiful, brilliant Charlotte Simmons, a sheltered freshman from North Carolina."[1]

I remember watching Wolfe being interviewed on TV when the book first came out. Much was made about the research he did at schools like Stanford University and the University of Michigan in preparation for the writing of this book, including first-person accounts of frat parties and keggers. He must have been a big hit, especially if he showed up wearing one of his trademark white suits. Not exactly undercover research, but who can question the methods of the man legendary as the master of detail?

In his countless book tour interviews, Wolfe acknowledged that based on his research and firsthand experience, the setting of his story and the wild sexual exploits of his characters were very much the norm on today's college campuses. His story and characters were simply a reflection of our times. However, most young women (and men) growing up in the midst of our pornographic culture aren't nearly as naive and sexually inexperienced as Charlotte by the time they enter college—which makes her such a remarkable character.

A book reviewer who would have been a peer of a real-life Charlotte had this to say in the book's comments section on Amazon.com:

> I was interested in reading this book because Tom Wolfe did a good chunk of his research at the large public university I went to. … In fact, he was at a fraternity party I was at one night, conducting this "research," and one of my sorority sisters is mentioned in his "thank yous" for the help she gave him while getting acclimated on our campus. . . Do 18-year-old girls like this even EXIST anymore? I'd love to meet one. I don't know now, nor have I ever known, a girl as naive as Charlotte Simmons' character, even when I was 18 myself. I'm sure a few exist somewhere, but she certainly does NOT represent the average female freshman in the U.S. It's as if Tom Wolfe decided to write a story about a girl from HIS high school generation entering into today's college atmosphere. [sic].

For those of us far removed from our college days—Wolfe in his early seventies when he wrote his book, I in my late forties writing mine—it's nearly impossible for us to understand what it's really like to step into the shoes of today's teenage college students. Those of us with older children (my boys are now thirteen and twenty-one) have the added handicap of thinking that just because we're their parents, we know and understand what's going on in the minds of our kids and their peers.

To make matters worse, our pride and egos won't let most of us believe that our own kids could possibly be involved in anything that violates our own values and belief system, like looking at porn. We think to ourselves, "I can't believe what kids today are doing. Our kids would never do that!"—as if they possess some kind of genetic "Get Out of Jail Free" card. Sounds nice. But from my own personal experience, that's rarely the way it really is. Most children aren't nearly as naive as their parents think they are.

GROWING UP IN PORN NATION

So what are we to make of this next generation of emerging young adults? If they have little in common with the innocent and naive Charlotte, does that mean our world is run amok with promiscuous rebels? Of course not, thank God. But if most young people are sitting somewhere in the middle, then the real question to ask is this: how is growing up in our Porn Nation influencing their lives, both in the way they view themselves and in the way they see and act toward others in relationships?

That's a difficult question to answer, but a quick read of some recent studies and statistics combined with anecdotal stories gives us some clues. In 2002, a huge study of the sexual beliefs, attitudes, and behaviors of almost 13,000 teens and adults ages 15–44 was conducted by the Centers for Disease Control.[2] The results showed clear signs of a growing chasm between the generations when it comes to sex. A key finding was that adolescents are aggressively redefining what sex and intimacy are. One area that clearly illustrates this "shift" of the line of sexual normalcy is oral sex. For example, with more than half of 15- to 19-year-olds reporting they're having oral sex, the study reported teens viewing it so casually they feel it needn't even occur within the confines of a relationship. Some say it takes place randomly under tables in the lunchroom, at parties, even with multiple partners. That's a huge shift from previous generations.

David Walsh, a psychologist and author of the teen-behavior book *Why Do They Act That Way?* says the brain is wired to develop intense physical and emotional attraction during the teenage years as part of the maturing process. But he's disturbed by the casual way sex is often portrayed in the media, which he says gives teens a distorted view of true intimacy. Sex—even oral sex—"just becomes kind of a recreational activity that is separate from a close, personal relationship. When the physical part of the relationship races ahead of everything else, it can almost become the focus of the relationship," Walsh says. As a result, teens are "not then developing all of the really important skills like trust and communication and all those things that are the key ingredients for a healthy, longlasting relationship."[3]

A survey of more than 1,000 teens conducted with the National Campaign to Prevent Teen Pregnancy resulted in *The Real Truth about Teens & Sex*, a book by Sabrina Weill, former editor-in-chief at *Seventeen* magazine. She points out that teens' casual attitudes toward sex—particularly oral sex—reflect their confusion about what is normal behavior. She believes teens are facing an intimacy crisis that could haunt them in future relationships. "When teenagers fool around before they're ready or have a very casual attitude toward sex, they proceed toward adulthood with a lack of understanding about intimacy," says Weill. "What it means to be intimate is not clearly spelled out for young people by their parents and people they trust."[4] This became crystal clear to me during a recent conversation I had with a college student after one of my Porn Nation campus lecture events. "Mr. Leahy, you talk a lot about how we're all looking for true intimacy. I'll be honest—I'm not looking for intimacy, I just want to have sex!" This wasn't a tongue-in-cheek comment. He was dead serious.

Invariably, separating sex from relationships for the sake of the act itself is a form of sexualization and objectification of both individuals involved. In fact, it almost sounds like a milder if voluntary form of dissociation, "a state in which some integrated part of a person's life becomes separated from the rest of the personality and functions independently."[5] In conversations I've had with former sex industry workers, especially former strippers and porn stars, this was a common practice they utilized that enabled them to perform day after day. It's also been documented as a common coping strategy for survivors of rape, incest, and other forms of violent sexual abuse.

So why focus on the isolated act of oral sex when discussing the changing sexual attitudes, beliefs, and behaviors of teens? Well, for one thing, it gives us a glimpse into how a few of the interrelated parts of our "perfect storm" have worked together to cause a shift in cultural attitudes toward sexuality. For example, we know that most teens believe intercourse is the only thing that constitutes sex, while other sexual activities do not.[6] In fact, roughly half of young teens who have had oral sex or sexual intercourse were involved in a casual relationship; 67% of those who have engaged in casual relationships often do so "to satisfy a sexual desire."[7] The Kaiser Family Foundation found that 60% of teens cited that "many of their friends had already done it" as a factor influencing their decision to have sex,[8] and a similar number believed that their peers think having sex by age 15 is socially acceptable.[9]

THE ASSAULT ON TEENAGE GIRLS

It's pretty common knowledge among teens today that oral sex is most often performed by teenage girls on teenage guys rather than the other way around. How much of that is a reflection of the pressure on girls to act out sexually for the sake of impressing or pleasing the guy, or his or her peers, is anyone's guess. The recurring theme in our media of a woman needing to be sexy or sexual enough to get the guy is a time-worn message. Fifty-nine percent of girls age 12–19 agree that society tells them that attracting boys and acting sexy is one of the most important things girls can do.[10] Teenagers say messages from the media make them feel that casual sex is normal and suggest that all teens are preoccupied with sex. "I feel like I see more commercials about casual sex than I do about how important it is to have a family and how important it is to be in a marriage instead of having sex with people from a bar," says Shanae Sheppard, a seventeen-year-old senior from Owings Mills, Maryland.[11] A female student I spoke to after one of my talks put it this way: "I was raised to believe that sex is something you saved for your husband. But when I got here to the university, I learned pretty quickly that being sexual and hooking up with guys was almost a prerequisite. It's just part of today's campus culture. Like the stuff we grew up seeing in the media and our music, only now we can live it out loud and nobody blinks an eye."

Our sociosexual pathology has become the fuel that drives our hypersexual media (or is it the other way around?). Add to that the anytime, anywhere access we now have via enabling technologies to Web sites and social networks that feed our sexual proclivities, and you have an unrelenting form of real-time sex "education" for the masses. With the media inexorably lured to the $150-billion-a-year teen consumer market, it's no wonder kids today say that when it comes to sexual content, they feel like they're soaking in it. For instance, girls see over 400 advertisements per day telling them how they should look.[12] Similarly, the *Washington Times* observed, "Young people are sexualized at an earlier and earlier age. . . . Stars like Britney Spears and Christina Aguilera have long been criticized for exploiting their sexuality for profit. The next generation can already be seen emulating its older sisters—literally."[13]

As these trends continue, my greatest fear as a recovering sex addict is contemplating just where the line of sexual normalcy will move to next. How long before even graphic and twisted expressions of sexuality (like pedophilia, rape, or S&M) gain acceptance into the mainstream? As unrealistic as that may sound, we wouldn't be the first great society to go down that path. The latter days of the Roman Empire are infamous for sexual depravity on a massive scale.

People like myself who fed on pornographic images for decades know firsthand just how far one can push that line of demarcation in their own lives. But it was different for us because most of us did it to ourselves. Today, the rapid mainstreaming of all things sexual has taken the freedom of choice away from individuals and made it into a force-fed diet. So we trade our history of sexual conservatism and naivety for a new kind of sexual freedom and worldly awareness that commercializes sexuality and turns it into a form of self-abuse. And as we look around to see if innocence still exists, all we find are "barely legal" porn sites and girls "going wild" for their first time. It's no wonder our friend the book reviewer couldn't relate to a character like Charlotte Simmons. Sadly, so few of them exist anymore.

A TRUE STORY

Not long ago I received an e-mail from Erin, a college student who heard me speak at the University of Louisville. As often happens once I've "broken the ice" by sharing intimate details of my own life on stage, others begin to experience the freedom found in sharing their own stories, most often one on one with trusted friends. In this case, even though we've never talked or met face to face, for a moment in time I became one of those trusted friends to Erin. Because her story is so typical of what I hear from college co-eds as I travel and speak, with her permission I've shared Erin's story with thousands of college students during a talk I sometimes give about how much sexuality and spirituality have in common. Unfortunately, her story is far from unique. In our Porn Nation, when the two distinct worlds of abuser and abused come together, the end result can be heartbreaking. Fortunately for Erin, she not only survived the wreckage of her young life, but she went on to discover new freedoms she never knew existed before. Her e-mail reads:

Dear Michael,

I just wanted to thank you for speaking at U of L. I just recently became a Christian, and seeing what porn is and thinking about how I used to live my life. Well, I realized I was porn, and your speech just broke me down. I was a girl searching for love in all the wrong places, dressing to get attention. Even if it was negative, it was better than nothing. I had always felt empty and alone.

My parents divorced when I was 12, and I always blamed my dad for the way I lived my life. I thought if he had given me more attention I wouldn't have turned out so screwed up. But after hearing you speak, I realized it was all me. My dad and I hadn't spoken in about 2yrs, and that night I called him up crying, saying I was sorry.

I am only 20yrs old and have had at least 15 partners. I was raped in the 8th grade, and ever since that I always thought that guys only wanted one thing, and I gave it to them freely. That's how I was trying to fill the emptiness I had inside of me, to have a quick feeling of love. I would have 5 guys in my life at one time. I would sleep with each of them and then decide how they can benefit me. The one that gave me good sex, I would use him for booty call. The one good with foreplay, that's all he was used for, etc. I looked at guys as sex toys, someone to please me. And I always had to be in charge. When people say porn, I would think of a dirty old man. I never thought of myself like that.

When I turned 18, I sat my dad down and told him I wanted to be a stripper. He asked why. I said I needed the money, and apparently guys like my body and think I'm hot so why not. All my dad had to say was, "Let me know which clubs so I don't have to see you." After that conversation, I really felt that my dad didn't care.

That's when I was looking for a guy to fill my void of love from my dad, and I was searching but I could never find it. The last "relationship" I was in, the guy was cheating on his girlfriend with me. When I found out, it hurt because I thought I was the only one. But yet I still wanted to be with him.

When I realized how consumed with jealousy I was, I just kind of gave up, and God started working in my life. I wanted to feel filled and wanted God in my life, but just a little bit because I was so afraid He would judge me and wouldn't accept me as one of His children because I wasn't "pure." But once I told God I was sorry for everything from having sex before marriage to blaming Him for my parents' divorce, I started to realize I couldn't survive without His help.

When God found me, it was like the greatest love anyone could have ever given me. I want to thank you so much for bringing all of these things to my attention. I had them stored away and forgotten, but you made me consciously think about how I used to live, and how I don't feel like that anymore, and how awesome God is.

Thank you so much. Signed, Erin

Stories like this abound in our society. It's as if we've truly lost our way in our quest for sexual freedom and self-discovery. And if we weren't the ones harming ourselves, there was always someone nearby who could snatch our innocence away forever. How did we get that way? How do people become so captivated by one of the most private and personal matters of human existence that the obsession over it ends up destroying its very presence in their lives and in the lives of others?

It does happen. It happened to me. And it can happen to you too, if it hasn't already. In fact, long before any of us ever became addicts we all struggled with this condition, a kind of sex syndrome. We all slowly started losing control.

CHAPTER

11

Introducing
SEX SYNDROME

Nearly forty years ago, I stumbled upon pornography for the first time. It was 1969 and I was eleven years old. About a year later, I started masturbating to pornography and porn-inspired thoughts of sexual fantasy. In essence, I was starting to form a "relationship" with the material whereby I would use it to alter my mood or state of mind. Whenever I was bored or stressed out or depressed, or was just looking to escape and entertain myself, masturbating to porn and sexual fantasy was always an option.

Over the next thirty years, my relationship with porn ebbed and flowed. At times, it was a big part of my life and consumed a large part of my conscious thoughts. Yet at other times, it was practically nonexistent. Most of the time, it was just kind of "there," subtly present in the background of my life. For the most part I functioned as a normal, balanced human being. I was responsible, hardworking, fun loving, compassionate, and a bit goofy—but normal, not obsessive or compulsive about my sexuality or anyone else's.

When I did look at porn I considered myself to be a recreational user of a rather harmless albeit embarrassing form of entertainment. It was my guilty pleasure, and the rationale I used to justify my use of the material was that it wasn't hurting anyone. Just a cheap, pleasurable form of entertainment.

Sure, there were times when I would obsess over a picture or a person. And yes, I'd always hide the fact that I looked at porn from others. I knew that Patty wouldn't approve of what I did in secret, and neither would my family or friends or my employer. In most people's minds, porn was still taboo and evoked images of a dirty old man slipping into a seedy X-rated movie theater wearing only an overcoat and shoes. Or the perverted Peeping Tom sneaking around the neighborhood at night, looking through people's windows to watch them undress. I knew I was neither of those things, but who would ever believe me or understand that once I told them what I did? Better to just keep it a secret.

CROSSING THE LINE

Over the years, getting access to porn became easier and easier. The more I fed my porn habit, the greater my desire was to look at the material. Not only that, but in between the times I would look at porn, I would catch myself thinking about the images. Sometimes I would get sexually aroused just at the thought of slipping off and looking at porn. As time went on the lightheadedness, or high, I would normally feel when simply using porn and masturbating occurred to a lesser degree. To achieve the same effect, it took looking at real people. This was especially true whenever I traveled and stayed in hotels. I could always count on having a line of sight from my room into other rooms with partially closed blinds or drapes. The adrenaline rush I got looking at the pictures on voyeur Web sites was always stronger for me than the other stuff I looked at, but it was even stronger when I became an active participant in the act itself.

Looking back on years spent in recovery, I've tried to figure out when I crossed "the line" from recreational use into compulsive use and addictive behavior. The Internet was clearly my rocket fuel that kicked things into high gear and kept my thoughts of fantasy energized. But I believe it was when I started moving from passive viewer to active voyeur that I began sliding down that slippery slope, the fall from grace one hears addicts speak of so often. That's when I passed the point of no return. Nothing came close to that exhilaration, the high, the buzz that I felt for hours on end.

From the very moment the thought or idea of acting out as a voyeur entered my mind to the fading rush after orgasm, I was high. With magazines, the high was brief—typically less than an hour. With videos, more intense but still relatively short—a few hours at most. The Internet was a huge leap, with "sessions" lasting anywhere from several hours to an entire morning, afternoon, or evening. Acting out in real life as the voyeur or exhibitionist was so intense I would literally start shaking and could be on a low-grade buzz for days before as I planned my exploits. I would later discover that the only thing that came close was being in an affair 24/7 with another woman who happened to also be a sex addict.

Crossing the line from recreation into addiction didn't happen overnight. It was a series of events, a shift in my sexual attitudes and beliefs that would occasionally erupt as sexual acting-out behaviors. It all took time, lots of time. I was redefining my own personal views about what was and wasn't acceptable sexual behavior starting from the time I was first aware of my own sexuality, which wasn't long before my first exposure to porn. Over the next twenty-five years those actions and attitudes escalated into a self-destructive series of sexually compulsive and addictive behaviors. In other words, it took me two and a half decades to become a sex addict and the next five years for my life to become un-manageable enough to lose it all.

As anyone who's lived with an alcoholic or drug addict can tell you, recognizing that person as an addict is not that difficult once they start losing control and their life starts coming unraveled. It's painful to see, like watching a train wreck unfold in slow motion. Hearing the excuses about another lost job, bailing them out of jail, or just seeing them high again are dead giveaways that even a child can recognize. Even before they become an addict, most people close to them can see it coming.

But that's alcoholism or drug addiction. What about the quiet build-up of insanity that characterizes behavioral addictions like sex addiction? Most of the time everything seems normal on the outside, save an occasional inconsistency in character or an isolated incident that gets quickly rationalized or dismissed. What was going on inside of them all those years when the water on the surface appeared calm but the disturbances deep below indicated a tsunami was picking up steam?

UNDERSTANDING WHAT LIES BENEATH

To help us gain a better understanding of what goes on beneath the surface during that pre-addictive state, I want to introduce a new term—*sexual compulsivity syndrome*, or "Sex Syndrome" for short.

Before I go any further I want to clarify that Sex Syndrome is not an officially designated or recognized medical disorder or disease. Rather, it's a phrase I've coined to describe a very real state or condition that clearly exists but up until now has been ignored by the mental health community. I've used this term to help myself and others understand the process one typically goes through as an individual that can lead to unwanted sexually compulsive or addictive behaviors, or sexual addiction. But it doesn't apply only to individuals. Sex Syndrome can also describe a sociosexual pathology that affects a group of people or an entire society when the group or society exhibits its symptoms and characteristics.

Sex syndrome as I define it is a pathological state we enter when our capacity for sexual pleasure and intimacy decreases as our exposure to intense sexual stimuli (like Internet pornography) increases. The condition involves both behavioral and biological factors, and taken to the extreme, it can result in sexual addiction.

To understand Sex Syndrome, you first need to have a basic understanding of how the brain, the most powerful sex organ in our body, processes sexual stimuli. We now know, for instance, that there is a cocktail of chemicals in the brain that energizes attraction and sparks romance.[1] Moreover, those chemicals are totally different from the blend that fosters deep love and long-term attachment.

One of those attraction/romance chemicals is dopamine, a neurotransmitter that creates intense energy, exhilaration, focused attention, and motivation to win rewards. It's triggered by, among other things, novelty, pornography, and sexual arousal. A different chemical, oxytocin, is a hormone that promotes a feeling of connection, bonding, and attachment. It's produced and released by the brain when we hug our spouses or children, and when a mother nurses her infant. There are others also, like serotonin and adrenaline, that play more of a supporting role. But it is in this sandbox of love potions that pornography comes to play.

Physiologically, in normal "love" relationships with real people, we typically move from the dopamine-drenched state of romantic love through various stages of increased intimacy to (if we're lucky) the relative calm and quiet of an oxytocin-induced attachment. But if we or our partner has formed a relationship with pornography and uses the material on a regular basis to induce fantasy-driven orgasms, our "relationship" with porn never leaves the attraction stage. It's always about getting off. So as pornography repeatedly triggers intense sexual arousal, our brain produces more and more dopamine, keeping us trapped in an intense cycle that mimics the early stages of infatuation, romance, and lovesickness. Overstimulate the brain with dopamine long and often enough, and the brain will adapt by increasing its tolerance levels. The result of increased tolerance is desensitization, similar to what an alcoholic or drug addict experiences after repeated use and abuse of their drug of choice.

Over time, as more sexual stimulation is required to get the same "high," the user starts seeking out new and different ways to increase the brain's production levels of dopamine. For the budding alcoholic or drug abuser, that may mean using greater quantities of the same drug or switching over to more potent drugs—beer to wine, wine to hard liquor, weed to cocaine, coke to crack or methamphetamine—to experience the same high they used to get.

It works the same way for a sex addict in the making—magazines to videos, couple to group sex, just watching to becoming an active participant. Setting and crossing boundaries, starting and promising yourself you'll stop, then starting all over again. Sex Syndrome is a scary place to be because you really don't think of yourself as being unhealthy or getting sick. You tell yourself and convince others that you're normal, there's nothing wrong with it, everyone's doing it. "It's harmless fun," you tell yourself. "Nobody's getting hurt." But you can't see the long, slow slide. You don't see what's really happening to you because you're partial and biased and far too invested in your past to ever really want to change.

As you can see, the Law of Increase/Decrease discussed earlier plays a major role in both the establishment of Sex Syndrome as well as its escalation into more harmful forms of sexual addiction. What you feed grows, and what you starve dies. If you continue to feed the brain ever-increasing amounts and varieties of intense sexual stimulation, the craving for a dopamine-drenched high grows.

However, the brain's ability to increase tolerance levels along the way to prevent overstimulation creates a quandary for the typical user. As they are surrounded with milder yet unsatisfying forms of sexual stimuli in our pornographic culture, they are constantly reminded of the need to quench their growing sexual appetites. The result is an ongoing sense of sexual dissatisfaction that can only be dealt with by either a) suppressing the growing desire for sex, or b) seeking out new ways and methods of satisfying their sexual desire. As long as the relationship between pornographic sexual stimulation and experiencing sexual satisfaction continues, the use of artificial sexual stimulants like pornography and out-of-bounds sexual behaviors (prostitutes, strip clubs, massage parlors, etc.) will only serve to increase their sexual compulsivity. With each new exposure, the brain builds tolerance, increasing the need for greater stimulation.

As we learned earlier, The Law of Increase rarely takes effect without the Law of Decrease creating an opposite and equal reaction (Newton's Law). Sex Syndrome is no exception. The desensitization one experiences as tolerance levels increase comes as a result of overfeeding your dopamine intake receptors. But "what you starve dies," and what's really being starved during this process is healthy intimacy with a healthy person in the context of a healthy relationship. In this case your primary sexual relationship is with an inanimate object like a picture or a video or a disengaged sex worker. Sexual intimacy has become all about taking with no giving, and the focus of your attention is really on you. As your sense of belonging and acceptance by others is being ignored, or starved, your sense of self and significance decreases. Increased isolation from real relationships is one of the unintended by-products.

As Sex Syndrome gives way to sexual addiction and compulsivity, the unmanageability of it all starts to sink in and the shame and guilt that fuel the addictive cycle become well entrenched. Unhealthy sexual attitudes and behaviors not only skew the individual's moral and relational compass, but also provoke self-condemnation and wreck self-esteem.

While it's doubtful that Sex Syndrome will ever be recognized by the American Psychiatric Association as a mental disorder—any more than they've been willing to acknowledge that sexual addiction exists (see the next chapter)—both are very tangible and real conditions for millions of people and their loved ones living in our Porn Nation. Most people who are experiencing the early and middle stages of Sex Syndrome see themselves as individuals who are still in control of their life and their relationships. But if the latter stages of Sex Syndrome resemble a place where the fog is just starting to roll in and cloud their judgment, in sexual addiction the ship is truly lost at sea and the captain hasn't a clue where he or she is.

CHAPTER

12

AM I a SEX ADDICT?

It's always interesting to me to see different people's reactions when I tell them I'm a recovering sex addict.

"Sex addict! Cool, I know a bunch of guys that are sex addicts. Ya know, they just have a higher sex drive than most people. In fact, I'm kinda like that myself!"

"Sex addict! You know, I think my son's a sex addict. I found porn on his computer the other day. That's the third time we've had to talk to him about it."

"Sex addict, huh? Give me a break! There's no such thing. Just a bunch of people who have weak character and lack of self-control playing the victim, if you ask me."

"Sex addict. Hmmm. Sounds serious. So, I need to know something. You haven't, like, sexually abused any young children or anything, have you? Or stalked any young girls in chat rooms, like those guys on TV's "To Catch a Predator"?

Over the ten years that I've been involved in sexual addiction recovery, it feels like I've heard and seen it all. In fact, turn on the TV and you're bound to catch an earful yourself. From sex addicts and their spouses being interviewed by Oprah Winfrey, who says that sexual addiction is America's number one addiction, to certain sex therapists and psychiatrists denying that such a thing even exists, wide-ranging opinions abound.

Then it should come as no surprise that the American Psychiatric Association, the organization that publishes the controversial *Diagnostic and Statistical Manual of Mental Disorders*, or DSM, has yet to officially recognize sexual addiction as a mental disorder. That hurts the estimated 16 to 21 million people in the United States who are sexually addicted[1] because the guide is used worldwide by clinicians and researchers as well as insurance companies, pharmaceutical companies, and policy makers.

Sexual addiction and those affected by it have a certain stigma attached to them by society and certain medical circles that resembles the early days of treating alcoholism or attention deficit disorder. To add insult to injury, without its inclusion in the DSM, insurance companies who use this manual as a guide have been reluctant to provide insurance coverage to companies and their employees for a disorder they can claim doesn't exist.

Is sexual addiction real or some mythological disorder? Numerous experts in the medical field who support its diagnosis describe it as being in many ways similar to other addictions, where the behavior or activity comes to be used as a way to manage mood or stress and may become more severe over time. Those like myself and my family and millions of others who have lived through the nightmare and continue to live with the consequences have little doubt that sexual addiction is real and incredibly destructive.

I have vivid memories of my time spent "in the bubble" of my addiction to porn and sex, complete with the requisite outbursts directed at anyone who dared question my activities. I've made incredibly stupid choices and stood before my loved ones emotionless, ready to discard fifteen years of marriage and two precious boys for a mirage of what I foolishly thought would be satiable sex. I've taken great risks of arrest and embarrassment, all for another high, another rush of dopamine and adrenaline. Once you've been an addict, you know your addiction is real and really dangerous. Once its risks and consequences are thoroughly understood, sexual addiction may one day be recognized as one of the most dangerous of them all. But for now it is too easily dismissed as a joke or with a flippant "boys will be boys."

WHAT DOES SEXUAL ADDICTION LOOK LIKE?

Sexual addiction is among the least understood of all addictions. Dr. Patrick Carnes, the world's foremost expert and pioneer in the area of sexual addiction and recovery, defines sexual addiction as any sexually related, compulsive behavior that interferes with normal living and causes severe stress on family, friends, loved ones, and one's work environment.[2] It's also described as a progressive intimacy disorder characterized by compulsive sexual thoughts and acts.[3]

Others talk about it more in terms of having an unhealthy sexual dependency. The Mayo Clinic uses *compulsive sexual behavior* for sexual addiction, and defines it as "an overwhelming need for sex" and describes a sexually addicted person as "so intensely preoccupied with this need that it interferes with your job and your relationships.... You may spend inordinate amounts of time in sexually related activities and neglect important aspects of your day-to-day life in social, occupational and recreational areas. You may find yourself failing repeatedly at attempts to reduce or control your sexual activities or desires."[4] However you choose to define it, sexual addiction is seen universally as an unhealthy or pathological relationship between an individual and their sexual thoughts and behaviors.

The latest research in this field gives us a clearer picture of who sex addicts are. It's estimated that 3 to 6% of the US population, as many as 15 million people, are sexually addicted.[5] Other estimates put the number slightly higher at 6 to 8% of the population, or 16 to 21 million people.[6] Either way, that's a lot of people—about the same number as those who struggle with alcoholism.

Sexual addicts come from every ethnic, religious, and socioeconomic background. Most come from severely dysfunctional families. Eighty-seven percent belong to a family where at least one other member of the family has another addiction.[7] Research has also shown that a very high correlation exists between childhood abuse and sexual addiction in adulthood. Ninety-seven percent of sexual addicts reported experiencing emotional abuse, 83% sexual abuse, and 71% physical abuse.[8]

While sexual addiction is generally believed to primarily affect men, it remains unclear whether one gender has a higher incidence than the other. Research by Dr. Patrick Carnes shows that approximately 20% of all patients seeking help for sexual dependency are women. (This same male-female ratio is found among those recovering from alcohol addiction.) As once was the case with alcoholism, many people cannot accept the reality that women can become sexual addicts. One of the greatest problems facing female sexual addicts is convincing others that they have a legitimate problem.[9]

INDICATORS OF SEXUAL ADDICTION

So how do you know if you or someone you love suffers from sexual addiction? While an actual diagnosis for sexual addiction should be carried out by a mental health professional, the following behavior patterns compiled by Dr. Patrick Carnes can indicate its presence.[10] (See Dr. Carnes's excellent Web site www.sexhelp.com for additional helpful information.) You can also go to the appendix at the end of this book to take the twenty-five-question Sexual Addiction Screening Test, or go online and take the test at www.mysexsurvey.com.

The SAST is a diagnostic tool developed by Carnes and other healthcare professionals that generally correlates with the behavioral patterns below. Of course, individuals who see any of these patterns in their own life, or in the life of someone they care about, should seek professional help.

1. *Acting out: a pattern of out-of-control sexual behavior.* Examples may include compulsive masturbation, frequent use of pornography, chronic affairs, exhibitionism, dangerous sexual practices, prostitution, anonymous sex, compulsive sexual episodes, or voyeurism.

2. *Experiencing severe consequences due to sexual behavior, and an inability to stop despite these adverse consequences.* Some of the losses reported by sexual addicts, and the percentage of sex addicts reporting such consequences in their own lives, include:

- Loss of partner or spouse (40%)
- Severe marital or relationship problems (70%)
- Loss of career opportunities (27%)
- Unwanted pregnancies (40%)
- Abortions (36%)
- Suicidal obsession (72%)
- Suicide attempts (17%)
- Exposure to AIDS and venereal disease (68%)
- Legal risks, ranging from nuisance offenses to rape (58%)

Even understanding that the consequences of their actions will be painful does not stop addicts from acting out. They often have a willfulness about their actions, and an attitude that says, "I'll deal with the consequences when they come."

3. Ongoing desire or effort to limit sexual behavior. Addicts often try to control their behavior by creating external barriers to it. For example, some move to a new neighborhood or city, hoping that a new environment removed from old activities will help. Some think marriage will keep them from acting out. An exhibitionist may buy a car in which it's difficult to act out while driving. Others seek control over their behavior by immersing themselves in religion, only to find out that while religious compulsion may soothe their shame, it does not end their acting out. Many go through periods of sexual deprivation during which they allow themselves no sexual expression at all. Such efforts, however, only fuel the addiction and address the symptoms rather than the root problem.

4. Sexual obsession and fantasy as a primary coping strategy. Though acting out sexually can temporarily relieve addicts' anxieties, they still find themselves spending inordinate amounts of time in obsession and fantasy. By fantasizing, the addict can escape reality to live in a make-believe world of images and past experiences. Together with obsessing, or maintaining an almost constant level of arousal, the two behaviors can create a kind of analgesic "fix." Just as our bodies generate endorphins—natural antidepressants—during vigorous exercise, our bodies naturally release peptides when sexually aroused. The molecular construction of these peptides parallels that of opiates like heroin or morphine, but are many times more powerful.

5. *Regularly increasing the amount of sexual experience because the current level of activity is no longer sufficiently satisfying.* Sexual addiction is often progressive. While addicts may be able to control themselves for a time, inevitably their addictive behaviors will return and quickly escalate to previous levels and beyond. Some addicts begin adding additional acting-out behaviors. Usually addicts will have three or more behaviors that play a key role in their addiction—masturbation, affairs, and anonymous sex, for instance. In addition, 89% of addicts reported regularly "bingeing" to the point of emotional exhaustion. The emotional pain of withdrawal for sexual addicts can parallel the physical pain experienced by those withdrawing from opiate addiction.

6. *Severe mood changes related to sexual activity.* Addicts experience intense mood shifts, often due to the despair and shame of having unwanted sex. Sexual addicts are caught in a crushing cycle of shame-creating and shame-driven behavior. The few moments of guilt-laden euphoria eventually devolve into strong feelings of shame that then drive the addict to find sexual escape once again.

7. *Inordinate amounts of time spent obtaining sex, being sexual, and recovering from sexual experiences.* Two sets of activities organize sexual addicts' days. One involves obsessing about sex, time devoted to initiating sex, and actually being sexual. The second involves time spent dealing with the consequences of their acting out: lying, covering up, shortages of money, problems with their spouse, trouble at work, neglected children, and so on.

8. *Neglect of important social, occupational, or recreational activities because of sexual behavior.* As more and more of addicts' energy becomes focused on relationships that have sexual potential, other relationships and

attributes—family, friends, work, talents, values—suffer and atrophy from neglect. Long-term relationships are stormy and often unsuccessful. Because of sexual preoccupation and intimacy avoidance, short-term relationships become the norm. Sometimes, however, the desire to preserve an important long-term relationship, with spouse or children, for instance, can act as the catalyst for addicts to admit their problem and seek help.

In my own life, I experienced every one of these behavior patterns at one time or another, and all of them simultaneously while I was addicted. Of course, in the midst of my addiction I was in denial that most or any of these symptomatic behaviors were either present or all that serious. But as the disorder progressively got worse, the symptomatic behaviors became more pronounced to family and friends, as did the related consequences. The existence of a few or even one of these behavior patterns could point toward any of a wide variety of causes or mental disorders. However, taken together as symptomatic behaviors in one individual, the probability that a sexual addiction exists is highly likely.

THE CYCLE OF ADDICTION

Addicts have tried often to stop, and failed. Their behavior generally conforms to a cycle:[11]

1. *Preoccupation—the addict becomes completely engrossed with sexual thoughts or fantasies.* Often I would "zone out" as I was engrossed in thoughts of fantasy, even when other people were nearby. If this happened while I was alone, it was easy to lose track of time. A half hour became an hour, and an hour turned into several hours. At times while preoccupied with sexual thoughts, I would suddenly come to realize I was late for a busi-

ness meeting or an appointment. In that case, I would typically resume my sexual thoughts or fantasies after the "interruption" was over and I was alone again to indulge once more.

2. *Ritualization—the addict follows special routines in a search for sexual stimulation, which intensify the experience and may be more important than reaching orgasm.* I had many rituals and routines, all very specific and planned out. Some rituals consumed me and required that I ignore or block out everything else in my life—my job, my wife and family, other obligations. Many rituals were simply integrated into other daily routines, like checking out Internet porn sites after reading my work e-mail, or revisiting those porn sites and printing out certain pictures before leaving the office for home.

3. *Compulsive sexual behavior—the addict's specific sexual acting-out behaviors. Examples of these are compulsive masturbation, indulging in pornography, having chronic affairs, exhibitionism, dangerous sexual practices, prostitution, anonymous sex, compulsive sexual episodes, and voyeurism.* This is the area where you play a game with yourself regarding what you deem to be acceptable and what is "out of bounds" behavior. The more you expose yourself to certain behaviors, the more compulsive you grow and desensitized you become to acting-out activities. And the more desensitized you become, the more apt you are to cross the line into behaviors you once considered unacceptable.

4. *Despair—the acting out does not lead to normal sexual satisfaction, but to feelings of hopelessness, powerlessness, depression, and the like. Risk factors for the addict include having unstructured time, circumstances that require self-direction, and demands for excellence, because they all push the addict toward restarting the addictive cycle.* The feelings of guilt, shame, and despair would always come

rushing in on me immediately after acting out. I would despise myself for what I had done and always make a promise to never do it again. As I wrestled with intense negative feelings of self-hatred and disgust, I would start to escape by becoming preoccupied with a whole new series of sexual fantasies. There was always a trigger or something just around the corner that would con me into thinking that this time my Great Escape would take away the pain.

To be sure, sexual addiction is controversial, and it is important to realize that some people latch onto this label instead of accepting personal responsibility for the choices they've made in life, choices that may have hurt themselves and others. Once I could see the damage I'd done to myself and others because of my addiction, it was only natural for me to also accept full personal responsibility for my past choices and accompanying consequences. But whether the addict is at a place in his or her recovery to accept responsibility for their actions or not, sexual addiction is a very stark reality for millions of men and women in this country.

For some, it's a living hell that instills intense feelings of hopelessness and helplessness in the face of our society's onslaught of sexual images and messages. Yet for others, it's been an important part of a life-long journey, a difficult lesson on the importance of self-respect and the respect of others. For those of us on the other side of hopelessness, it's taught us valuable lessons about ourselves and others as whole human beings—physical, emotional, spiritual people who possess an immeasurable capacity to rise above our circumstances in order to remake ourselves into better people. We are the ones who chose to get well, and now we have a story to tell and a message of hope to share with everyone else.

PART 3

THE TRUTH ABOUT THE NEW YOU

13

Defining Moments:
DO YOU WANT
to GET WELL?

In every person's life there are defining moments, times when the entire course and direction of a person's life can change instantly. These are critical junctures, forks in the road where one's destiny lies in a solitary decision. Do I stay or do I go? Marry him or say no? Take the job or look for another? Call her back or lose the number? Defining moments require a decision, a choice, a move in one direction or the other.

I believe that every addict will come face to face with at least one defining moment in his or her life, one opportunity to choose whether to get well or stay sick. Most of us will have multiple opportunities to turn things around, both for our lives and the lives of others around us—family, friends, and loved ones. The circumstances will vary and the situations will all look different, but the question will always remain the same.

"Do you want to get well?"

To the casual observer, it seems like a simple enough question with an even simpler predictable response. "Yes, of course I do! Just look at what a mess I've made of my life! Of course I want to get well."

That answer makes sense to everyone but the addict. To the person still lost in a fog of lies and self-denial and feelings of entitlement, getting well is a threat to life as they've known it. Getting well means taking a hard look at your life and possibly even admitting that you're wrong. Getting well means losing the battle, giving up control, and trusting others to help you direct your life. Getting well means betraying and maybe even losing your best friend, that thing you've been turning to for a long time that's helped you get through good times and bad—your coping mechanism whenever you're stressed out and feel like you're under attack.

Who will you turn to the next time you get stuck in a hard place in a relationship and feel like you can't breathe? Or when those sad and hurtful feelings come crashing down on your life and your heart begins to break? Does getting well mean you will feel all of that pain without anything or anyone to medicate you? Does it mean you have to face yourself, your painful past and present shortcomings, without any means of escape? If all of this is a part of getting well, then you might just as well stay sick and ride out the present storm.

This is the way an addict thinks. This is why so many people look at addicts' lives and their self-destructive ways and just walk away shaking their heads, mumbling something to themselves like, "I can't believe he's doing this to himself. What is he thinking?" Or, "How can she be so selfish? Can't she see how she's hurting her family?" The truth is, she probably can't. And no, he's not really thinking straight. All addicts are compulsive, pathological liars. They lie to others and they lie to themselves. The sicker they are, the more they lie. And the more they lie, the harder it is for them to recognize what is true and what is real. That is why most addicts have to hit bottom before they'll ever seek help, before they'll ever really want to get well. Hitting bottom means being broken and starting to see the truth from the lies. It's a wake-up call where all of the sudden you start to really see and feel the consequences of your actions. It is the best thing and the worst thing that can ever happen to an addict and their loved ones. It's death and new life all rolled into one. And it hurts like nothing else.

The first time I remember being faced with the question, do you want to get well? my answer was a resounding "Yes!" It was buried in an avalanche of tears and conveyed with a deep sense of sorrow and remorse for what I had done.

I was sitting in my pastor's office early on a Saturday morning with my brokenhearted wife of thirteen years holding my hands and sitting by my side. The night before, Patty had asked and I had confessed that I was having an affair. Now we were asking a trusted friend for help. Outwardly, it must have looked to both of them like I was a broken man who was truly sorry and was willing to do whatever it took to save his marriage. And I was sincere, at least at that moment. But then a couple of days passed. My relationship with my wife and kids was in critical condition, and the tension and stress that created in our home were practically unbearable. *How do I handle this? How do I cope with these feelings of failure and loss?* My unfaithfulness, a broken bond of trust and mutual respect, a future together that is now uncertain. It didn't take long before I was back on the phone with my affair partner, self-medicating the wounds with my drug of choice.

So it went for months and months. Sorrow, remorse, and brokenness followed by escape, fantasy, and acting out. Then I would get caught. A new round of confessions, of promises to myself and to them, "Never again!" But it was always just a matter of time before "again" would happen. Even my best lies and most elaborate stories couldn't hide the truth. I got sloppy, and then I quit caring. *Catch me once again. Remind me how horrible a person I am. Just don't leave me. I'll do whatever it takes. Just don't leave me. Because I love you.*

Those were the words I spoke to both Patty and Teresa. I wanted them both. I needed them both. I couldn't imagine living the rest of my life with one but not the other. Patty was my wife. We had built a life and a family together, and everything worked. I couldn't imagine not waking up to her each day. But Teresa was my fix, my drug of choice. Without my Great Escape, how would I cope? How would I survive if I finally had to feel my pain and my emotions? Who would I turn to?

Of course, it never dawned on me that Patty was the one I needed to turn to. In fact, turning to Patty to release the feelings and emotions I had only been sharing with pornography, then later with Teresa, my "porn with skin on," would have been the key to building a whole new level of intimacy with my wife. It could have happened years earlier. It should have happened before we got married.

But I didn't want to get well. I knew I was sick back then, at least a little sick. You know what they say—you're only as sick as your secrets. Before we were married, I had a decade of sexual secrets built up inside of me. I was sure that if anyone ever found me out, if anyone ever really knew me, they would reject me. I would be abandoned, left alone to face my greatest fear—being unloved and forsaken. The stakes were high back then, or so I thought. If I told Patty the truth, I risked her rejecting me and not marrying me. Or I could just be quiet, keep a secret a little while longer, and deal with it on my own. *After all,* I thought, *married life will solve my problems. Who would ever want to look at porn after marrying such a beautiful woman? We can have sex as often as we want. Who wants to look at pictures anyway when you can have the real thing?*

Fifteen years and many lies and secrets later, the stakes got much higher—two beautiful boys, countless family and friendship relationships, a twenty-year career, a beautiful home in the suburbs, a solid repu-

HEAL Your BODY by CHANGING Your MIND

Whether your goal is to recover from a full-blown sexual addiction or to rid yourself of some unwanted sexual attitudes, beliefs, and behaviors that are more symptomatic of Sex Syndrome, the paths to recovery and healing look very much the same. The only difference is the sense of urgency one typically has as an addict who has hit bottom.

But whatever the goal, this journey can only begin when you humble yourself enough to ask others for help. That means you—not your spouse or your parents or a friend—pick up the phone or walk into a counselor's office to say you're not well and ask for help. Until you can do that on your own, nothing in your life will change.

The journey continues by rejecting lies and false beliefs, developing a plan for healing, and persevering on the long but rewarding road to recovery.

CONFRONT THE LIES

Before I ever called a counselor on my own (Patty and others had always done it before as a condition of my being able to stay in the marriage), I had a lot of practice meeting with and lying to counselors and recovery group members. So my first order of business was to confess to my new counselor that I had lied to all the other counselors in the past. He didn't seem very surprised at the news. I did the same thing in my first meeting with my new recovery group. They just shrugged their shoulders like I was citing the obvious. From those first meetings onward, I knew that success in my recovery was going to depend on my ability to be honest with others and with myself. No more lies. It sounds good, but it was much harder than I thought.

For the first time in my life, I was trying not to lie—about anything. I had never really given it much thought before. Lying had become a way of life for me. Not blatant lies—those were too obvious. I preferred the little white lies. Or even better, lies of omission. "Don't ask, don't tell." I seemed to sleep better after telling (or not telling) those. My lies were subtle, gradual—a little twist of the truth here and a slight turn on reality there.

I remember my first lie. It had to do with pornography. It was a lie of omission. I simply chose not to tell my parents about the picture of the nude woman I had seen that day, the first day of my thirty-plus-year-long relationship with pornography. I had no reason to believe that I would get in trouble by telling them. My parents were usually very loving and understanding toward me. My dad may have had a drinking problem, and he may have lost his temper and punted me around my bedroom at times, but it's not like I was subjected to constant physical or emotional abuse.

We were a loving family, a model family in many ways—at least on the surface. But we weren't exactly honest with one another. Dad never owned up to the fact that he had a drinking problem. And Mom always made nice about it, so concerned with keeping the peace, with keeping us safe. So ours was a family of little white lies, lies of omission, of avoiding the truth and putting your best face forward. We all learned to escape facing the truth in our own ways. My way was through porn, and later, sex. It worked for me. And it was easy to hide. And if I ever got caught, I could always avoid the inevitable pain and embarrassment of the moment by telling a lie.

I once got caught red-handed for drilling a hole in the upstairs bathroom door in our home in Spokane. It was the bathroom my sisters used. My parents confronted me about it, and I lied and said I knew nothing about it. The door got fixed, and nothing was ever said to me about it again. That's kind of the way things were for us. We lied to one another. It seemed to work as a way to maintain the peace.

On the surface, recovery from sexual addiction looks like it's about stopping your acting-out behaviors. But it goes much deeper than that. It's really about separating the truth from the lies, because addicts have spent most of their lives getting the two all mixed up until we can no longer tell one from the other. One of the most valuable things I learned in recovery was that as a result of living a life of lies, every addict develops a faulty core belief system. It's what lies at the root of any addiction or self-destructive behavior.

Core belief systems are the sum of our assumptions, our judgments, and the viewpoints that we hold to be true about ourselves and others. In other words, it's the filter we use to interpret the world around us and inside of us. It's our truth, but for the addict it's based on lies.

That's important to understand because behaviors are the product of a person acting on those beliefs in order to meet a basic human need or to get something they want or desire. Everything works out great as long as what you believe to be true really *is* true. But in reality we end up making a lot of poor choices in life by acting on false beliefs. It's a recipe for failure.

For example, if you were sexually abused as a child by a parent, and all the while they told you this is how all parents express their love for their children, chances are pretty good that you'll grow up believing that to be true and acting toward others based on that truth, when in reality nothing could be further from the truth.

According to Patrick Carnes, there are four core beliefs that most sex addicts hold to be true. They are:

- I am basically a bad, unworthy person.
- No one would love me as I am.
- My needs are never going to be met if I have to depend on others.
- Sex is my most important need.[1]

One of my faulty core beliefs that got established very early on was that sex was my most important need. As a result I ended up sexualizing most of my relationships. For me, sex equaled love and acceptance. It also equaled status and manhood in the eyes of my peers. Along with athletic ability, sexual prowess became an important part of my identity and the basis of my self-esteem. As I was growing up, the more sexual I was with others, the better I felt about myself.

Another false belief for me was that no one would love me as I am. I thought that if anyone really knew the real me, including the sexual things I did in private, they wouldn't love me. Instead, they would reject and abandon me. This was a strong influence in my repeated decisions to keep my porn habit a secret from everyone, beginning with my parents and ending with my wife. But in the end, all it did was add the fuel of guilt and shame to the addictive cycle. Because I felt guilty and shameful about what I did, as well as unlovable, I would turn back to porn or act out sexually to numb the pain I was feeling. And the cycle would start all over again.

DEVELOP A PLAN FOR HEALING

As I went on doing the hard work of recovery through counseling and time spent getting honest in group therapy and 12-step groups, I came to realize it wasn't enough just to get some accountability to help me stop my self-destructive behaviors. I needed to begin to think differently about myself and others, and to replace the lies with the truth. I needed to integrate good habits and healthy behaviors into my daily routine. So I had to focus on changing the largest, most powerful sex organ in my body—my brain. My mind was where the battle raged. How I thought about myself as a sexual being helped to form my sexual attitudes and behaviors. And getting honest before others about how I thought, how I felt, and how I acted helped me to uncover those faulty core beliefs. But how could I change my mind? Could I ever hope to think differently about myself, or was I stuck with this recording in my head telling me the same old lies over and over again?

The very thought of changing my mind seemed like a daunting task at first. I had heard ugly rumors of a dramatically low percentage of sex addicts who were experiencing long-term sexual sobriety. In recovery-group speak, that was our main measure of success—no sex with self or others outside of a committed relationship (ours had the added caveat of "committed marriage relationship," being that I was involved in a faith-based group). The overwhelming challenge came in facing this dilemma: how does a sex addict detox or come off of using sex as a drug of choice when our society is saturated with sex at every turn?

I'd heard about guys going off to these retreat centers for six months to "dry out" by isolating themselves from society's sexual temptations. That idea never made much sense to me. I mean, what happens when you reenter society? I even ran across some 12-step fanatics that spoke of their "scorched earth" policy of recovery, always looking down, never looking directly at a woman. You've gotta be kidding me! How bizarre! I knew there had to be a better way.

I didn't necessarily like what I saw other people doing, so I designed my own detox program. There's an old saying we had in the computer industry: garbage in, garbage out. I thought about that a lot during my recovery in addition to the maxim, What you feed grows, and what you starve dies. So one day I did the unthinkable. I cut the cable on my TV. I even did it in the fall, just before football season. Talk about going cold turkey. My friends and family didn't really understand why I resorted to such extreme measures. Some even got mad at me for doing it, as if I were passing judgment on them for continuing to watch. I didn't really care what they did; I just knew I had to cut mine off for a time. There were too many images, too many triggers that invariably led to my acting out. I would have gotten rid of my TV altogether, or at least moved it out of the den, had it not been that I owned the largest production tube TV made at that time. It was a behemoth at 450 pounds. So I turned it into a photo collage of my kids instead.

About the same time I cut the cable on my TV, I also got rid of the Internet on my home computer. I was never tempted to look at porn on my work computer since they monitored our usage and I had high-speed Internet access and a powerful computer at home anyway. But the temptation to surf porn sites was too great since I lived in an apartment by myself. So off they both went, and it stayed like that for over a year. I must say, I've never been so productive with my time, and never thought so clearly.

After a year of no TV and no Internet, I started slowly getting back online and using the TV again, but this time I had accountability software on my computer and found myself watching TV a lot less. Instead

I spent more time outside exercising and doing things with my boys. I was also spending more time developing friendships with others. And at night, I started turning to a new favorite hobby of mine: reading. It was hard to beat a comfortable easy chair and a good book. I found no better way to fight this disorder and to turn the "garbage in, garbage out" axiom on its head than by putting good stuff into my mind and body—healthy food instead of comfort food and healthy thoughts and ideas instead of brain candy like porn.

ON THE ROAD TO RECOVERY

I kept seeing counselors and going to group meetings, but now it was less frequent. I developed a new set of friends, some of whom agreed to hold me accountable for my actions and thoughts. Of course, the quality of my recovery has always been in direct proportion to my willingness to be honest with myself and others. But starving myself of the sexual images and ideas that helped to build and reinforce my faulty core beliefs was just as essential to my healing as was filling the vacuum it created with positive images and more wholesome thoughts about others and myself. One day at a time, and often one minute or one thought at a time, I fought to replace the lie with the truth: That we all are wonders of creation. That people are inherently valuable. That if I'm willing to respect and honor others, I too am worthy of being respected and honored. Somehow, some way, what I was doing was working. I was thinking differently about myself and others.

What I didn't realize at the time is that I was literally "rewiring" my brain. New research in the area of neuroplasticity is showing us that there are many ways in which the brain is able to reorganize itself by forming new neural connections throughout life. As Sharon Begley, author of the book *Train Your Mind, Change Your Brain* puts it, "It's possible to change the structure and function of the brain, and in so doing alter how we think and feel."[2] In fact, "The brain can adapt, heal, renew itself after trauma, and compensate for disability."[3]

That was good to know, because in a way I had been traumatizing my brain for years by exposing it to a barrage of increasingly toxic sexual images. But once I started to break down my behaviors into component parts, beginning with whatever feelings or emotional states I was in or what I was doing at the time that triggered my thoughts of sexually acting out, I could then devise alternative courses of action that would remove me from those triggers in the first place. I started feeding and growing new thought patterns as I starved and killed off the old ones. And wherever my mind went, my body soon followed.

Ridding myself of old, unwanted sexual behaviors and replacing them with a new set of healthy habits emerged from a kind of psychological warfare I was having with myself. I've lost my fair share of battles along the way, but I feel like I'm winning the war. A big motivator for me to continue fighting the fight has been my boys. I desperately want them to have a healthy dad whom they can count on for the rest of their life. And now that I'm remarried to Christine, I've found that love and true intimacy can be reborn and even flourish in the aftermath of our shattered dreams.

But I found that even good intentions like maintaining healthy family relationships could only take you so far on the journey to wholeness. There needed to be something more, a greater cause or purpose than myself that I could draw strength from when the going got tough. I was feeling and acting like a better person, but was I really changing on the inside? Or was this just an extreme makeover of the same old me? Who was this person who had it all but ended up throwing it all away, and what was his purpose in life?

HEAL Your SOUL by CHANGING Your HEART

Being involved in a small group of guys who all struggled as sex addicts was probably the most transformational thing I've ever done. The group I hung out with the most was a combination of group therapy and 12-step.

We used a faith-based recovery group workbook developed by Dr. Mark Laaser[1] that I still believe is one of the best small group resources ever developed for sexual addiction recovery. Our group was led by a knowledgeable counselor who helped us keep our exchanges confidential and on track. But what really got me was the honest air of humility I felt every time I walked into that room. And that wasn't hard to create. After all, this was the weekly gathering of the Sex Addicts' Club! How much more humbling and embarrassing could it possibly get?

Getting to the meetings was one thing, but once I stepped inside I knew it was safe to share whatever it was I needed to say. Nothing else I've ever experienced in a small group of people has ever come close.

I know now that being connected with a group of guys who struggled just like I did had a lot to do with my successful recovery. Over the years that I was involved with this group, we shared a lot and discussed a wide range of issues directly related to our addiction.

FINDING GOD

Because we identified ourselves as a faith-based group, the subject of God came up a good bit. We were always being challenged to consider the role that our "higher power" played both in our becoming an addict and in getting well. Stuff like surrendering your will to God, confessing to God and others the exact nature of your wrongs, trusting God to remove your character defects. Lots of God stuff. The problem was, I still wasn't sure how I felt about God. We hadn't exactly been on speaking terms for some time now, and I still wasn't very clear about who I thought He really was to begin with.

Growing up in a religious home where I went to church all the time because I had to, but never understood why, didn't exactly give me a clear picture of who God was. It was just what we did on Sundays. As far as I could tell, God lived in a church and somehow had eyes to see everything we did. He had a Son, Jesus, who came and died for our sins, and one day we were all going to die and either go to heaven or hell forever. That was about it. In between birth and death there were a lot of rituals we were supposed to do, and the main way to please God was to not commit any of the big mortal sins and do more good than bad. And, of course, keep going to church.

I never was very clear about what it took to get into heaven after I died, but I always figured I was doing pretty good on the balance sheet of good works versus bad. So God to me was like this Super Dad: judge and jury, disciplinarian, and Santa Claus all wrapped in one. Jesus was a mystery to me. We never talked about Him outside of the church or my religion classes in grade school. I figured He was a historical character who inspired people to want to do good.

I guess the closest thing I had to compare to God was my dad. He was always there to provide for us and love us and take care of our basic human needs. But my dad wasn't exactly the poster child for healthy intimacy between a father and a son. Most of the time I found him to be busy, distracted, emotionally disconnected, or otherwise unavailable. As I got older I realized that he was an alcoholic, but everyone just ignored it and worked around it. I guess we all came up with our own methods of coping with my dad and his drinking problem.

If there really were a God, I figured He must be a reflection of my dad. When my dad passed away several years ago, what made me the saddest was that I never felt like I really knew him. Here he was, blood of my blood. I desperately wanted to be close to him like I was with my mom. She and I had always been like best buddies, and my dad and I had our moments. But it was never the kind of relationship I had hoped for. Even as we grew closer throughout my adult years, there was something missing between us. It was intimacy. We never allowed ourselves to be fully known to each other. We always seemed to play it safe and mostly stuck to shallow topics of conversation. I blame myself just as much for that as I blame him. It's just the way we were with each other.

As I started venturing into the deeper recesses of my soul during my recovery, I came to realize that's also the way I treated God. Disconnected, playing it safe, not really making the effort to get to know Him. It was easy to ignore God, but whenever a crisis came up in my life I'd call His name. "Help me, God!" Kind of like how I used to cry out for my parents to come rescue me, whether it was from falling on my bike or getting stuck up in a tree. But I wasn't a kid anymore. And with older parents now, we were the adults taking care of them. A crisis had emerged in my life and I had nowhere to turn to but God. I knew that it was up to me to approach Him, to humble myself and ask for help. But not just for the sake of getting unstuck. This time, I needed His forgiveness. I needed to say I was sorry for blowing it and for ignoring Him all these years. I needed to ask Him for a second chance.

On the night I thought about taking my life, the first thing I asked God for was to teach me how to talk to Him, to pray to Him. It felt like I had been running from Him for so long that I didn't really know where to start. I wanted to know what I could do to communicate and connect with Him. I knew He was there, but I had no idea how to initiate a relationship with the God of the universe. The way I had approached God in the past was very ceremonial, very fake—with rote prayers and words that didn't mean a whole lot to me. As a Christian living my adult life in the Bible Belt I discovered there was a lot of status to be gained by being public about your faith. So I learned years ago how to pray out loud and sound really good and holy and righteous. But now, the mere thought of praying like that made me sick to my stomach. I was well beyond trying to look good. I yearned for a real connection.

Eventually, I found myself just talking to God in a conversational way. No prettying up words or trying to sound all high and mighty. My conversations with God involved getting away to some place quiet, usually while out taking a walk in the woods somewhere, and just sharing the concerns, the joys, and the trials that burdened my heart. And then I'd shut up and listen. Sometimes I could sense God was with me and sometimes I couldn't. But it didn't bother me when I didn't sense His presence. His silence didn't mean that He wasn't there; it just meant that He was silent.

The more time I spent reaching out to God, the more I wanted to know about Him. It was that principle at work again—what you feed grows, and what you starve dies. I found an old Bible I had for years but had stopped reading, opened it up, and started reading it again. It was pretty worn and marked up, a telltale sign of a time when I used to take my spiritual health much more seriously. It reminded me of how important God had been to me back when I was much younger.

Now I started bringing my Bible with me whenever I'd go off to pray. A lot of times God would communicate to me by prompting me to read certain parts of Scripture. I used to think about the Bible the way I thought about textbooks when I was a student in college—something I had to study and drag around to class. But reading it the second time around with a fresh new perspective somehow made the stories come alive. For the first time in my life, I could see the character of God coming through, and it touched my heart.

I wanted to learn more about this God of the Bible I was rediscovering, so I started looking for a church that could teach me about God. But this time I wasn't in it for show. I didn't want to end up in a place that was all about rituals and symbolism and social status. I just wanted a place where I could approach God wearing jeans and a T-shirt and not feel out of place. I finally found a place like that just outside of Atlanta. All of the pieces had fallen into place for me to finally discover the truth about me and about God and about who He says that I am.

KNOWING THE TRUTH

One of the first verses of Scripture I looked up in the Bible was the one I thought of that day I discovered the truth about my affair partner. It's the one that says, "You will know the truth, and the truth will make you free";[2] only I learned that wasn't the whole passage. I thought it was important to understand what it meant because somehow God had made it clear to me that the truth that would make me free wasn't the truth about her but the truth about me.

I finally found that verse in one of the Gospels, the book of John. The Gospels were supposed to be significant because they recorded first-person accounts of the life of Jesus Christ, the man who claimed to be God and later rose from the dead after being put to death on a cross. That verse was actually spoken by Jesus. This is the full context of what He said:

> So Jesus was saying to those Jews who had believed Him, "If you continue in My word, then you are truly disciples of Mine; *and you will know the truth, and the truth will make you free.*" They answered Him, "We are Abraham's descendants and have never yet been enslaved to anyone; how is it that You say, 'You will become free'?" Jesus answered them, "Truly, truly, I say to you, everyone who commits sin is the slave of sin. The slave does not remain in the house forever; the son does remain forever. So if the Son makes you free, you will be free indeed. I know that you are Abraham's descendants; yet you seek to kill Me, because My word has no place in you."[3]

It took me a while to really understand everything that's going on here in relation to the bigger picture that the Bible paints. But several things really struck me about this exchange.

First, Jesus was talking to followers of His, people who already claimed to know Him and believe that He was the Son of God. Second, He makes them a promise: that if they continue to observe (or follow) His words (and instructions), they will be true disciples or followers of His. Then and only then will they be free, because they will know truth. In short, know Jesus and you will know truth.

Later on in that same book, Jesus goes on to claim, "I am the way, and the truth, and the life; no one comes to the Father but through Me."[4] Then He turns to Thomas, one of His disciples, and says, "If you had known Me, you would have known My Father also."[5] In other words, Jesus is equating knowing Him with knowing truth and knowing God, His heavenly Father. Heady stuff to say unless He really is who He claimed to be.

But the part that got my attention was the response He got from those He was speaking to. To paraphrase, "What do you mean 'you will be free'? I'm not a slave!" How many times have I used words like that to justify doing the wrong thing just because I could, or because I thought I could manage the outcome?

Jesus' response to His disciples then is the same response He gives you and me today: if you commit sin, you're a slave to sin. We all sin, which makes us all sinners, and all of us find ourselves guilty before God, who is holy and just.[6] Even though some sins may be dressed up to look like freedom, they really leave you in bondage and make you a slave. But God didn't just leave us in this sorry state without an escape route. While it's true that the penalty of sin is death, it's also true that Jesus came not to condemn us but to offer us forgiveness for our sins and the promise of eternal life.[7] That last one I'm still trying to get my arms around. But if there's one thing I know and can finally admit, it's that I'm a sinner who doesn't deserve forgiveness.

If the claims made by Jesus of Nazareth really are true (and I try to give the benefit of the doubt to anyone who rose from the dead), then this God the Father He speaks of is someone I want to get to know. I decided early on in my recovery to give God a second chance. And I'm slowly learning that God isn't a reflection of my earthly father; He's more like the perfection of the father I longed to know. His character contains an incomprehensible measure of love, and out of that flows forgiveness and grace and mercy and righteousness.

God's inspired Word, the Bible, has become both a comfort and a challenge to me. Some days I see it as a romance novel where the object of His love is me and the stories told there all point to His desire for our relationship to be reconciled and restored. On other days it reads like an incredible book of wisdom and knowledge on who God is and who He made me to be. And on those difficult days when I feel isolated and alone, or angry and unloved, I feel God's words penetrating my heart as if He Himself is holding me in His arms.

Recovery for me has been an ongoing journey to the very heart of God. Without the healing of my soul, I'm sure I would feel like a prisoner of my own process of behavior modification and cognitive therapy, lacking passion and purpose in my life. But when I started pursuing God, I discovered that He had actually been pursuing *me* all these years. I was just so full of myself I never noticed. My life is still filled with the consequences of my past sins, and the hurt and pain that I caused Patty and my boys and so many others is forever etched into my conscience. But as I've learned to accept God's love and forgiveness for my own sins, my soul gets stronger and I can feel myself changing from the inside out.

In the book of Ezekiel, God made a promise to His people, a promise that's available to anyone who chooses to love God and to continue in His word by following Jesus: "I will give you a new heart and put a new spirit within you; and I will remove the heart of stone from your flesh and give you a heart of flesh."[8]

Truth be told, we all live with damaged souls. Life is just like that—harsh, unforgiving, unloving. But our souls can and will be healed if we have a change of heart. Not the kind of change that comes from stuffing our feelings or disassociation or putting on a thin veneer of happiness. But the transformational change of a new heart, which we can only receive through a restored relationship with God through Jesus Christ.

Are you ready and willing to accept God's forgiveness for your sins? The exact nature of your past sins doesn't really matter. Nor does it matter that you'll definitely sin again. All that matters is that a new heart awaits you. Are you ready to be reconciled to God? Are you ready to become a minister of reconciliation to others in a world of broken relationships and wounded souls?

16

SEX GOD
RON JEREMY

Inviting God into your life to let Him remove your heart of stone and replace it with a new heart of flesh sounds like a deal that's too good to pass up. But sometimes, a little thing called unforgiveness can get in the way.

Over the years I've advised numerous men and women who struggle with sexual sin and sexual addiction and claim that they want to be free. Some are willing to go to almost any length just to distance themselves from these daily battles they wage with their very souls. Yet one problem keeps coming up for the vast majority of them, and it usually stops them dead in their tracks.

In the face of freedom and the opportunity to start anew, people who struggle with sexual sin or unwanted sexual behaviors have the hardest time forgiving *themselves*. It's truly disheartening to see so many good people choosing to stay in bondage due to unforgiveness. They don't believe that they deserve a second chance, that God's grace and mercy and forgiveness either don't apply to them, or worse yet that they're not worth more than the lies they've come to believe about themselves.

Case in point is my friend Ron Jeremy, legendary former porn star and veteran of over 1,600 adult films. Ron and I have been touring the country together for years now doing a series of porn debates on college campuses. Wherever we go the students treat him like some kind of sex god—even though these days he looks more like he does pizza and beer than porn.

A new understanding of the true spiritual cost of porn really started to hit home for me when Ron and I were together in Baton Rouge, Louisiana, several years ago to do a porn debate at Louisiana State University. It was just weeks after Hurricane Katrina had slammed into the Gulf Coast. Like the smothering heat and humidity that blanket Louisiana that time of year, we could sense the presence of death all around us as soon as we got into town. In Baton Rouge, the locals were no doubt thankful they were spared the worst of the storm. Yet, overnight, it had transformed this normally free-spirited college town into a giant morgue and medical triage facility.

That wasn't exactly the party atmosphere Ron and I had grown accustomed to encountering when visiting other campuses on the tour. By now, most students would have been abuzz and electrified in anticipation of watching a porn industry legend debate a recovering sex addict on the ethics of pornography. It had all the markings of a traveling circus freak show, symbolizing the very essence of the college party experience. But here at LSU, on this day, the atmosphere was far more subdued.

When we finally made it to the Alumni Hotel and Conference Center, we ended up hanging out in the hotel lobby with some extra time to kill before heading off to the debate. Before I knew it, Ron was engaged in some small talk with a slight-looking guy in his early thirties sporting a baseball cap with an "NBC News" logo on it. He was sitting in one of the overstuffed chairs that graced the lobby, surrounded by a bunch of expensive camera equipment.

"Hey, where can I get one of those hats?" Ron blurted out (I've noticed he blurts out a lot in public). The photojournalist obviously recognized him.

"Hey, you're Ron Jeremy, aren't you? You like the hat? Here, take this one. I'll get another one later on."

Pretty soon, I joined in the conversation, and it quickly changed focus from souvenir hats to stories about what this guy had seen and heard while on assignment in New Orleans.

His tone became somber. "Everywhere we turned, we saw dead people floating down these rivers that once were city streets. Block after block. At times it was just overwhelming."

Ron seemed ready to blurt out something again, but stopped short. I could tell he was also disturbed by the topic of discussion. His tone matched that of our new friend.

"I don't like to think about death," he said. "Just the thought of it bothers me. I'll admit, I'm scared of dying."

When I heard him say that, I was surprised. My initial reaction wasn't planned or staged. It was just automatic, and so I said the first thing that came to my mind.

"Really?!"

That was it. I didn't even think much of it when I said it. But it obviously spoke volumes to Ron. I mean, I really was surprised to hear him say that he was so scared to die. And evidently, he was just as surprised to learn that I wasn't.

"What? And you're not?"

"No."

"You mean you're not afraid to die?" His voice expressed disbelief.

I just shook my head and shrugged my shoulders. "No, not really."

He still couldn't believe my response. So in what I've come to learn is the patent Ron Jeremy tactic of continuing to rephrase the question until he gets the response he's looking for, he offered me another chance to change my mind by asking me the same question a different way.

"The thought of leaving all of this behind doesn't bother you? Of dying and leaving this world, all of your friends, your life just ending. That doesn't bother you?"

I simply shook my head once again and said, this time with a tinge of sarcasm, "No, the thought of leaving all of this behind doesn't bother me in the least. In fact, in a lot of ways, I'm looking forward to that day."

Now I could tell that Ron was really perplexed, especially at the nonchalant attitude I had toward the whole subject. I thought that was the end of our brief exchange on death and dying. But Ron surprised me yet again.

"I want to talk with you some more about that, later on when we have more time."

"Sure," I said, half expecting that we'd never have that conversation.

The following morning after the debate, I met up with Ron for breakfast in the hotel restaurant. After we sat down to eat following a visit to the breakfast buffet, there was the usual small talk and chatter about the weather, our flight times, the debate the night before. Then, much to my surprise, Ron picked up right where he'd left off. On the topic of death and dying.

"Hey, we've got a couple of hours before we have to leave for the airport. Did you bring a bathing suit?"

I nodded, trying not to visualize Ron and me in bathing suits while eating.

"There's a jacuzzi out by the pool. Let's go out there after breakfast and finish our conversation. I still want to talk with you about, ya know, death and dying and all that."

I about choked on my powdered eggs.

"Yeah, sure."

Before I knew it, there I was, sitting in a jacuzzi in Baton Rouge, Louisiana, next to Ron Jeremy, the hairiest former porn star in history. He was filled with a thousand questions about death and dying and heaven and hell and God. All of this was eating at Ron and he just wanted to talk about it. Now. So there we sat, in a pool of boiling water for nearly two hours, save the occasional interruption by a coed from across the street looking for his autograph. All in all, it was a truly surreal moment in my life, especially as the conversation turned to more personal subjects, like girlfriends and sexual intimacy and losing in love.

At several points, Ron would preface what he was about to say with the statement, "I know you could use this against me in the debates, but …" It was a rare demonstration of private vulnerability that I seldom saw from Ron. Of course, I never have divulged anything he's ever shared with me in private and never will, even if doing so would help me win the debates. I think he knew that about me already, given all the time we've spent getting to know each other. While his personal disclosures would make for some pretty compelling anecdotal evidence to further support my claims of the hidden dangers and long-term consequences of porn consumption, I think maintaining the mutual trust and respect we have for each other is of far greater importance.

At one point in our conversation while we were talking about heaven and hell, I looked him straight in the eye and asked, "Ron, if there is a heaven and there is a hell, where do you think you'd go?" I'm not really sure why I asked him that. It just kind of came out of my mouth.

"Oh, that would be hell," he quickly replied, chuckling and sounding half serious and half joking. I laughed with him for a moment, but before I could get another word out, he was spouting off about some other topic. I've thought a lot about that exchange and many others like it that Ron and I have had. I'm not sure why he thinks he's unworthy of going to heaven. Maybe he's like me, convinced like I once was that he's crossed the line with God and committed the unpardonable sin. Porn actor or adulterer—what's the difference? Or maybe he's not convinced that giving up his fame and his fans as a legend of the porn industry is worth the trade-off of knowing God. Perhaps it's a standoff—sex god Ron Jeremy versus the One True Sex God, the Creator of sex and the Author of life itself.

I know what that feels like too: when arrogance overtakes humility and you think of yourself as the center of the universe. Granted, Ron is a nice guy to hang out with, albeit pretty foul-mouthed at times. But I wouldn't want to spend a day in his shoes. Not with all the stress and pressure and demands that are put on a sex god, especially one who has to constantly live by the world's pornographic standards of sexuality. As a pop culture icon in a pornographic society, Ron is uniquely positioned to never have his deepest needs for love and intimacy met.

I'm well aware that Ron is every bit as loved by God as I am, and that he could be every bit as forgiven by God of his past sins as I have been. Yet when we believe in the lies and allow them to replace the truth, even the life-changing, life-saving reality of God's offer of eternal life can be hard to recognize. When I last asked Ron if he believed he'd end up in heaven or in hell when he died, his answer was no surprise to me. He thought he would probably go to hell. So I can totally understand why Ron is afraid of dying. I would be too if that's all I could see waiting for me at the end of my life.

Of course, he doesn't have to stay on that path. None of us do. You can always choose a different path that leads to a different destination. But you can't wish or will your way to a new destination if you're not willing to get off the same old path you've been on all your life. As much as he and I have talked about it, as of this writing, Ron and many others just like him still refuse to step off the path, to drop to their knees, to admit their way might not have been the best way. They don't want to change paths. The lies that got them there are keeping them there, but only because they let them.

There are many subtle consequences that can result from a lifetime of feeding on the lies and fantasy of pornography. But perhaps the greatest of these is the damage done to our spiritual selves. Because at some point, after immersing yourself in the lies for so long, the truth about your spiritual condition slowly fades away, seemingly out of view and beyond your reach. When that happens, it's easy to stop believing that a spiritual part of you even exists. And then the thought of turning back just becomes too painful an option to consider. Under the weight of shame and self-condemnation, your hope begins to fade. You feel completely alone. And it seems like no one really cares. You are dying inside. You are dying spiritually.

But the idea that it's too late to turn back to God, to be reconciled to your Creator and reconnected with your spiritual self, is the biggest lie of all. No matter how far the lies you've believed about yourself have carried you away from God, His love and forgiveness are more than able to bridge that gap and bring you into a relationship with Him. That's what a real sex God does.

So what about you? Are you ready to exchange the lies that have held you back all these years for the Truth of God that makes you free? No one will force it on you. It's up to you. It's always been up to you. Are you ready to experience the pure freedom of God's forgiveness through Jesus Christ? I did, and this was the Truth that finally set me free.

CONCLUSION

RECONCILED
and **RESTORED**

After spending about six years working on my recovery, I started traveling around sharing my story with others and talking about what I've learned. Over the last three years, this has included over 40,000 students on over one hundred college campuses. Since I always do a Q&A at the end of my talk, by now I've gotten pretty used to the responses: "I didn't know you could be addicted to porn"; "What should I do if my boyfriend is addicted to porn?"; "Isn't there an amount of this stuff you can look at without becoming addicted?" Those and many more. All good questions. I wish someone would have come to my campus to speak on this subject, although I can't say for sure how I would have responded.

Interestingly, though, the top three questions have nothing to do with sex or porn: 1) "How's your relationship with your wife?" 2) "How's your relationship with your ex-wife?" and 3) "How's your relationship with your boys?" After someone asks one of "the questions," everything gets quiet, as if their own hope for their relationship with a significant other, or reconciliation with a mother, father, brother, or sister, hangs on my answer.

At that point in the presentation, concern is no longer about free speech rights, or even whether porn is morally right or wrong. Ultimately, what people care about most are relationships. Which I suppose, in the end, is really my point. The health of our relationships with others, ourselves (self-esteem), with our spouse, kids, boyfriend/girlfriend, and the relationship we have with God: these are more important than porn, or alcohol or money or anything else we might be tempted to sacrifice them for. Relationships are real life. When we break our connections with others, we break connection with ourselves (experienced through guilt and shame) and ultimately break connection with God. This is why the moral law can be distilled down to a single imperative: Love the Lord your God with all your heart, soul, strength, and mind, and love your neighbor as yourself.[1] In the same way, this book really sharpens down to this one singular point: Relationships are life, and pornography puts these relationships in peril—everything else is just a footnote.

But I don't believe the moral law rules the universe; I believe that grace does, through the redemption provided by Christ. And regardless of how badly we've damaged or even severed these relationships, God is able, and more importantly *willing*, to bring reconciliation and restoration.

You see, long before I had the affair, I was slowly starving my relationship with Patty of intimacy. So when she realized that my affair with porn equated to thirteen years of mental and emotional unfaithfulness, our relationship started to crumble. Trust was ripped from the relationship, roots and all, with bitterness, anger, and resentment growing up in its place. Even after the divorce, our relationship played out largely in shouting matches, game playing, and continuous psychological warfare. She didn't like me and I didn't like her. But dislike turned to hate when she started dating Tommy, her boyfriend and soon-to-be husband, and started bringing him around the boys and me. Of course, the kids suffered as well, taking hits of emotional shrapnel anytime Patty and I fought. There were a lot of ugly scenes between us back then, and I was always ready to provoke more.

But once I hit bottom things began to change. It was slow at first, but real emotion began to circulate through me once again, thawing my heart and bringing with it a flood of sorrow for the pain I was inflicting on other people's lives. I still remember when Patty first commented to me about the change she and the boys were seeing in me. I thanked her but couldn't really explain or put into words what was going on.

One day, while pulling off Interstate 16 at Exit 32, the midway point between Atlanta and Savannah where Patty and I had been meeting for years to hand off the boys on visitation weekends, something inside of me was saying, "Now is the time. This is when you need to tell Tommy you're sorry and ask him to forgive you." It's something I had been thinking about doing for several weeks but still needed a few more years to mull over. I had been a real jerk to Tommy ever since I met him. He seemed like a real nice guy, and I knew he was good to my kids, but he had taken my place, and everything I had lost was now his and—God forgive me—I couldn't have hated him more for it.

But it was years later, and God had been taking me down the path of reconciliation in many of the relationships in my life. I had derived satisfaction in treating him like dirt for a long time, but it all seemed so foolish and mean-spirited now. As the boys climbed into the backseat of their car and Patty and Tommy started for the front, I called out to Tommy and we met near the rear of the car. The next thing I knew I was folding at the knees, telling him I was sorry, and asking him for forgiveness through a steady stream of tears. An intense wave of sorrow overcame me. It was as if for a moment I embodied the pain I had inflicted on him all those years. I'm thankful it was momentary—who can bear the full weight of their sin? We hugged each other, and through tears I saw the startled faces of my sons looking at us through the back window. Tommy accepted my apology. I knew he would. He was just that kind of guy and still is to this day. A good man.

As I was walking back to my car, I suddenly realized that my hatred for him was gone. Vanished! In an instant. All the anger, bitterness, and resentment had been stolen from my heart. I believe that God prompted me to do my part—tell Tommy I was sorry and ask him for forgiveness—and then He did His part: removed the stain.

The same process was repeated over and over again in other important relationships. Repentance, confession, forgiveness. Repentance, confession, forgiveness. Like going through spiritual detox, I could feel myself getting better and feeling freer each and every time. First with Tommy, then Patty, then the boys, then Patty's family. Her parents even ended up inviting me to use their cabin on those weekends when I had the boys. These were the same people who drove all night from Savannah years earlier to do an intervention on me as I continued to cheat on their daughter. I had always loved and respected Patty's parents. I just never expected to feel that love and respect from them again after what I had done.

The dictionary describes an icon as a person regarded as a symbol of something. Being regarded as a sports icon would be rather flattering; an icon for porn and sex addiction, less so. But as a spokesperson for sex addicts, I accept that—to a degree—that's exactly what I am: my life a symbol for the roughly 15 million adults in this country who struggle with addiction to sex and pornography. But my story—beginning with a mildly erotic deck of playing cards and moving up to high-speed cyberporn and then on to voyeurism, an affair, and then divorce—may also serve as a picture or analogy of our society on its sexual journey. As it's an analogy and not a prophecy, who can say if our culture as a whole will end up as I did, addicted to sex? But it could. Prophecies must be fulfilled, but analogies only need to instruct. As actions are taken, outcomes can always change. But if actions are not taken, I don't see how the truth of my story will not become the truth of *our* story, where I become a sex symbol of a different sort for our entire culture instead of just 15 million of its members.

And yet, as meaningful as it is odd to become a symbol and spokesperson for sexual addiction, I feel my life's greater value is as a symbol of God's grace, an icon of God's forgiveness, a modern-day prodigal son. Someone who demonstrates that no matter how lost you are and no matter what you've done, God can redeem you, your life, and your relationships. The universe is not ruled by the moral and religious law, which condemns us. It is ruled by grace for those who would freely receive it.

For the law was given through Moses; grace and truth were realized through Jesus Christ. (JOHN 1:17)

NOTES

Preface

1. Charles Babington and Jonathan Weisman, "Rep. Foley Quits in Page Scandal," *Washington Post*, September 30, 2006; Russell Jenkins, "Violent Pornography Blamed for Turning Boy Aged 14 into a Rapist," *The London Times*, March 24, 2006; Michael Janofsky, "Official Resists Extradition on Charge Involving Internet and Sex," *New York Times*, April 6, 2006; Ed Hayward, "Girls, 11 and 12, Post Nude Photos on Net," *The Boston Herald*, January 17, 2002; Elissa Gootman, "Father Sought to 'Swap' Girl, 4, for Sexual Abuse, Officials Say," *New York Times*, October 12, 2001.

Chapter 4

1. Sexual addiction expert Dr. Patrick Carnes, writing in his book *In the Shadows of the Net*, refers to this as our sexual arousal template. See Patrick J. Carnes with David L. Delmonico, Elizabeth Griffin, and Joseph M. Moriarity, *In the Shadows of the Net* (Center City, MN: Hazelden, 2001), 54.

Chapter 7

1. Lori O'Keefe, "Pediatricians Should 'Tune In' to Patients' Media Habits," American Academy of Pediatrics, *AAP News*, January 2001.

Chapter 8

1. "Sex on TV 4," a biennial study conducted by the Henry J. Kaiser Family Foundation, www.kff.org.
2. American Academy of Pediatrics, Committee on Public Education, "Media Violence," *Pediatrics* 108 no. 5 (Nov 5, 2001). http://aappolicy.aappublications.org/cgi/content/full/pediatrics; 108/5/1222.
3. Lori O'Keefe, "Pediatricians Should 'Tune In' to Patients' Media Habits," American Academy of Pediatrics, *AAP News*, January 2001.
4. Rebecca Collins, et al., "Watching Sex on Television Predicts Adolescent Initiation of Sexual Behavior," *Pediatrics* 114 no. 3 (2004): 280–289.
5. Al Cooper, David L. Delmonico, and Ron Burg, "Cybersex Users, Abusers, and Compulsives: New Findings and Implications," in *Cybersex: The Dark Side of the Force*, ed. Al Cooper (Philadelphia: Brunner-Routledge, 2000), 6.
6. Suzanne Vranica, "Reinvent the Wheel in 2004—Or Risk Being Flattened by It," *Wall Street Journal*, January 7, 2004.
7. Neil Malamuth and James Check, "The Effects of Aggressive Pornography on Beliefs in Rape Myths: Individual Differences," *Journal of Research in Personality* 19 (1985), pp. 299–320. For related information see C. Everett Koop, "Report of the Surgeon General's Workshop on Pornography and Public Health," *American Psychologist* 42 (1987): 945.

Chapter 9

1. Richard Jerome, et al., "The Cyberporn Generation," *People*, June 25, 2004. http://www.people.com/people/article/0,,658134,00.html.
2. National Coalition for the Protection of Children & Families, "Current Statistics," http://www.nationalcoalition.org/resourcesservices/stat.html.
3. Ben Feller, "Now I Know My Internet: More Nursery Schools Learn Online," *USA Today*, June 4, 2005.

4. Jerry Ropelato, "Internet Pornography Statistics," TopTenREVIEWS, http://internet-filter-review. toptenreviews.com/internet-pornography-statistics.html.

5. Rebecca Collins, et al., "Watching Sex on Television Predicts Adolescent Initiation of Sexual Behavior," *Pediatrics* 114 no. 3 (2004): 280–289.

6. National Coalition for the Protection of Children & Families, "Current Statistics," http://www. nationalcoalition.org/resourcesservices/stat.html.

7. Ibid.

8. "Nearly 3 in 10 Young Teens 'Sexually Active,'" NBC News, *People* Magazine Poll, January 19, 2005. http://www.msnbc.msn.com/id/6839072.

9. Sharon Jayson, "Survey: Many Teenagers Have Oral Sex," *USA Today*, September 9, 2005.

10. National Coalition for the Protection of Children & Families, "Current Statistics," http://www. nationalcoalition.org/resourcesservices/stat.html.

11. Ibid.

12. Ibid.

13. "Kids Stay Connected," *USA Today Snapshots*, January 5, 2004.

14. National Coalition for the Protection of Children & Families, "Current Statistics," http://www. nationalcoalition.org/resourcesservices/stat.html.

15. Marilyn Elias, "Cell Phone Use Booms, Despite Uneven Service," *USA Today*, March 14, 2004.

16. "40% of 15–19 Year Olds in the US Are Wireless Subscribers," report issued by International Data Corporation, December 2004.

17. Jennifer L. Schenker, "In Europe, Cell Phone Profits Go Up as Clothes Come Off," *The New York Times*, 4 May, 2004.

18. Daniel Terdiman, "Putting Flesh on Phones," Wired.com, http://www.wired.com/gadgets/wireless/news/2005/04/67165.

Chapter 10

1. Tom Wolfe, *I Am Charlotte Simmons* (New York: Picador, 2005), front flap.

2. Centers for Disease Control and Prevention, "Trends in Sexual Risk Behaviors among High School Students—United States, 1991–2001," *Morbidity and Mortality Weekly Report* 51 (2002): 856–859.

3. Sharon Jayson, "Teens Define Sex in New Ways," *USA Today*, October 19, 2005.

4. Ibid.

5. Dissociation, WordNet® 3.0, © 2006 Princeton University. http://wordnet.princeton.edu/perl/webwn?s=dissociation&o2=&o0=1&o7=&o5=&o1=1&o6=&o4=&o3=&h=.

6. Sharon Jayson, "'Technical Virginity' Becomes Part of Teens' Equation," *USA Today*, October 19, 2005.

7. "Nearly 3 in 10 Young Teens 'Sexually Active,'" NBC News, *People* Magazine Poll, January 19, 2005.

8. J. Davis, ed., "*Sex Smarts: Virginity and the First Time*," Kaiser Family Foundation, 2003.

9. National Coalition for the Protection of Children & Families, "Current Statistics," http://www. nationalcoalition.org/resourcesservices/stat.html.

10. The National Campaign to Prevent Teen Pregnancy, "American Opinion on Teen Pregnancy and Related Issues 2007," *Science Says* 31 (2007). http://www.teenpregnancy.org/works/pdf/Science_Says_31.pdf.

11. Sharon Jayson, "'Technical Virginity' Becomes Part of Teens' Equation," *USA Today*, October 19, 2005.

12. Centers for Disease Control and Prevention, "Trends in Sexual Risk Behaviors among High School Students—United States, 1991–2001," *Morbidity and Mortality Weekly Report* 51 (2002): 856–859.

13. "Mini-Britneys," *The Washington Times*, 3–9 May, 2004.

Chapter 11

1. *Lauren Slater,* "Love: The Chemical Reaction," *National Geographic*, February 2006.

Chapter 12

1. "The National Council on Sexual Addiction Compulsivity estimated that 6%–8% of Americans are sex addicts, which is 16 million–21.5 million people." See Alvin Cooper, Dana E. Putnam, Lynn A. Planchon, and Sylvain C. Boies, "Online Sexual Compulsivity: Getting Tangled in the Net," *Sexual Addiction and Compulsivity* 6:79–104.

2. Dr. Patrick Carnes, "Sex Addiction," SexHelp.com, http://www.sexhelp.com/addiction_definitions.cfm.

3. Michael Herkov, Ph.D., "What Is Sexual Addiction?" PsychCentral.com, http://psychcentral.com/lib/2006/what-is-sexual-addiction/.

4. Mental Health Center, "Compulsive Sexual Behavior," MayoClinic.com, http://www.mayoclinic.com/health/compulsive-sexual-behavior/DS00144/.

5. Carnes, "Frequently Asked Questions," SexHelp.com, http://www.sexhelp.com/addiction_faq.cfm#how-many.

6. Alvin Cooper, et al., "Online Sexual Compulsivity: Getting Tangled in the Net," *Sexual Addiction and Compulsivity* 6:79–104.

7. Carnes, "Frequently Asked Questions," SexHelp.com, http://www.sexhelp.com/addiction_faq.cfm#multiple.

8. Ibid.

9. Carnes, "Frequently Asked Questions," SexHelp.com, http://www.sexhelp.com/addiction_faq.cfm#male-female.

10. Carnes, "Frequently Asked Questions," SexHelp.com, http://www.sexhelp.com/addiction_faq.cfm#behavior.

11. See Patrick Carnes, *Out of the Shadows: Understanding Sexual Addiction* (Center City, MN: Hazelden, 1992).

Chapter 14

1. Patrick Carnes, *Out of the Shadows: Understanding Sexual Addiction* (Center City, Minnesota: Hazelden, 1992), 99–102.

2. Sharon Begley, *Train Your Mind, Change Your Brain* (New York: Ballantine Books, 2007).

3. Ibid.

Chapter 15

1. Dr. Mark Laaser, *Faithful & True Workbook* (Nashville: LifeWay Press, 1996).

2. John 8:32.

3. John 8:31–37, italics are mine.

4. John 14:6.

5. John 14:7.

6. Romans 3:10, 19, 23.

7. Romans 6:23; John 3:16–17.

8. Ezekiel 36:26.

Conclusion

1. Luke 10:27, abbreviated.

APPENDIX

APPENDIX A
Statistics

PORNOGRAPHY INDUSTRY

Unless otherwise noted, the statistics below are found in Jerry Ropelato, "Internet Pornography Statistics" (www.toptenreviews.com), and are drawn from credible news and business sources.

- At $13.3 billion, the 2006 revenues of the sex and porn industry in the US were bigger than the revenues of the NFL, NBA, and Major League Baseball combined.

- Worldwide sex industry sales for 2006 are reported to be $97 billion, more revenue than Microsoft, Google, Amazon, eBay, Yahoo!, Apple, Netflix, and Earthlink combined. China is the largest consumer with $27.4 billion, South Korea is second at $25.7 billion, Japan is next at $20 billion, and the US is fourth highest at $13.3 billion.

- Every second in the US, $3,075 is spent on pornography, 28,258 Internet users view pornography, and 372 Internet users type adult search terms into search engines.

- US sex industry income breakdown for 2006 (vs. 2005):
    - Video sales and rentals: $3.62 billion (down from $4.28 billion in 2005)
    - Internet: $2.84 billion (up from $2.5 billion)
    - Cable/PPV/in-room/mobile phone: $2.19 billion (up from $1.34 billion)

- Exotic dance clubs: $2 billion (unchanged)
- Novelties: $1.73 billion (up from $1.5 billion)
- Magazines: $950 million (down from $1 billion)
- Total: $13.3 billion (up from $12.62 billion in 2005)

- Child pornography generates $3 billion annually worldwide.

- 420 million: Total number of porn pages

- Pornographers currently release over 13,000 adult movies per year—more than 25 times the mainstream movie production. Every 39 minutes a new pornographic video is being created in the United States.

- Comcast, the nation's largest cable company, pulled in $50 million from adult programming in 2003. The big hotel chains like Hilton, Marriott, Hyatt, Sheraton, and Holiday Inn all offer adult films on in-room pay-per-view television systems. Adult movies are purchased by a whopping 50% of their guests, accounting for nearly 70% of their in-room profits.
  – CBS News Special Report, November 2003

PORNOGRAPHY CONSUMERS

- 1 of 3 visitors to all adult Web sites are women; 9.4 million women access adult Web sites every month.

- 20% of men and 13% of women admitted to accessing pornography at work.

- 72 million: The approximate number of unique visitors to adult Web sites in 2006, per month, worldwide.

- 40 million: The number of US adults who regularly visit porn Web sites.

- The largest consumer of Internet pornography is the 35–49 age group.

- In a Kinsey Institute survey, respondents were asked, "Why do you use porn?" 72% said they used porn to masturbate/for physical release. 69%—to sexually arouse themselves and/or others. 54%—out of curiosity. 43%—"Because I can fantasize about things I would not necessarily want in real life." 38% – to distract myself.

- A study of university computer networks by Palisades Systems found searches for child pornography at 230 colleges nationwide. The research revealed that 42% of all searches on file-to-file sharing systems involved child or adult pornography. The study also found that 73% of movie searches were for pornography and 24% of image searches were for child pornography; only 3% of the searches did not involve pornography or copyrighted materials.
  — Des Moines Register, April 1, 2003

- In May 2004 *BusinessWeek* printed the results of a ComScore Networks survey in which 44% of US workers with an Internet connection admitted to accessing an X-rated Web site at work in the month of March 2004, as compared to 40% of home users and 59% of university users.

- More than 30% of 1,500 surveyed companies have terminated employees for inappropriate use of the Internet, while only 37.5% of companies use filtering software.
  — *Websense Incorporated and The Center for Internet Studies, 2000*

- 38% of adults believe it is "morally acceptable" to look at pictures of nudity or explicit sexual behavior.

  — *Barna Research Group, "Morality Continues to Decay"*

- Incidents of child sexual exploitation have risen from 4,573 in 1998 to 112,083 in 2004, according to the National Center for Missing & Exploited Children.

  — USA Today Snapshots, "Reports of Child Exploitation Up," 17 February 2005

THE IMPACT OF PORNOGRAPHY

- 51% of US adults surveyed believe that pornography raises men's expectation of how women should look and changes men's expectations of how women should behave. 40% of adults surveyed believe that pornography harms relationships between men and women.

  — *Harris Poll, "No Consensus among American Public on the Effects of Pornography on Adults or Children or What Government Should Do About It,"* 7 *October 2005*

- 1 out of every 6 women grapples with addiction to pornography.

  — *"Internet Pornography and Loneliness: An Association?" Vincent Cyrus Yoder, Thomas B. Virden III, and Kiran Amin,* Sexual Addiction & Compulsivity, *Volume 12.1, 2005*

APPENDIX B

The Sexual Addiction Screening Test
Developed by Dr. Patrick Carnes, founder, Sexhelp.com

The Sexual Addiction Screening Test (SAST) was developed by Dr. Patrick Carnes and has become one of several diagnostic tools commonly used to help determine to what degree a person's sexual behaviors might have become compulsive or addictive.

To take the test, answer the twenty-five yes/no questions by circling the number of each question you answer "yes" to. Your score is equal to the total number of your "yes" responses. At the end of the test, you'll find a general assessment of what your score might mean with regards to your overall sexual compulsivity and sexual health. This test is in no way meant to be final or conclusive; it is just an early diagnostic tool.

Special Note to College Students: Go to www.mysexsurvey.com to complete a confidential online version of this SAST and become a part of the largest sex survey of its kind ever done just of college students. These survey results and their analysis will be the subject of a new book estimated to be published in 2009.

1. Were you sexually abused as a child or adolescent?
2. Do you regularly read romance novels or sexually explicit magazines, or regularly visit sexually explicit Web sites or chat rooms?
3. Have you stayed in romantic relationships after they become emotionally or physically abusive?
4. Do you often find yourself preoccupied with sexual thoughts or romantic daydreams?
5. Do you feel that your sexual behavior is not normal?

6. Does your spouse (or significant other[s]) ever worry or complain about your sexual behavior?

7. Do you have trouble stopping your sexual behavior when you know it is inappropriate?

8. Do you ever feel bad about your sexual behavior?

9. Has your sexual behavior ever created problems for you and your family or friends?

10. Have you ever sought help for sexual behavior you did not like?

11. Have you ever worried about people finding out about your sexual activities?

12. Has anyone been hurt emotionally because of your sexual behavior?

13. Have you ever participated in sexual activity in exchange for money or gifts?

14. Do you have times when you act out sexually followed by periods of celibacy (no sex at all)?

15. Have you made efforts to quit a type of sexual activity and failed?

16. Do you hide some of your sexual behavior from others?

17. Do you find yourself having multiple romantic relationships at the same time?

18. Have you ever felt degraded by your sexual behavior?

19. Has sex or romantic fantasies been a way for you to escape your problems?

20. When you have sex, do you feel depressed afterwards?

21. Do you regularly engage in sadomasochistic behavior (S&M, i.e., sex with whips, leather, spanking, pain, etc.)?

22. Has your sexual activity interfered with your family life?

23. Have you been sexual with minors?

24. Do you feel controlled by your sexual desire or fantasies of romance?

25. Do you ever think your sexual desire is stronger than you are?

ABOUT YOUR SCORE: The Sexual Addiction Screening Test (SAST) is a diagnostic tool on which data continues to be collected. As a result, cutoff scores may change depending on how people respond to the test. Your results are simply meant to be guidelines and suggestions and in no way replace a comprehensive assessment from a trained professional. If you feel you have a problem with sexually compulsive or addictive behaviors, regardless of your score, we suggest you seek professional help.

LOW RISK—0 to 8 "yes" answers. You may or may not have a problem with sexually compulsive behavior. You are in a low-risk group, but if your sexual behavior is causing problems in your life, confide in a trusted friend for support and personal accountability and consider seeking the help of a professional counselor or healthcare specialist with experience in this area who can conduct a further assessment.

AT RISK—9 to 18 "yes" answers. You are "at risk" for your sexual behavior to interfere with significant areas of your life. If you are concerned about your sexual behavior and have noticed consequences as a result, you should confide in a trusted friend for accountability and seek out the help of a professional counselor or health-care specialist with experience in this area who can conduct a further assessment.

HIGH RISK—19+ "yes" answers. You are at the highest risk level for your sexual behavior to interfere with and jeopardize important areas of your life (social, occupational, educational, etc.). It is essential that you share this in confidence with a trusted friend willing to keep this confidential yet hold you accountable for your actions. We also strongly recommend that you discuss your compulsive and addictive sexual behaviors with a professional counselor or health-care specialist experienced in this area of work to further assess the situation and assist you.

APPENDIX C
Recommended Reading and Other Resources for Recovery

The books, recovery groups, and resources listed below are intended to provide the reader with more information and a starting point from which they can begin their recovery. It is not intended to be a comprehensive listing of what is available.

RECOMMENDED READING

In addition to the books and articles cited in the endnotes, the following is a recommended reading list:

The White Book of Sexaholics Anonymous, SA Literature, 1989

False Intimacy: Understanding the Struggle of Sexual Addiction, Dr. Harry Schaumburg, NavPress, 1997

The Purity Principle, Randy Alcorn, Multnomah, 2003

Contrary to Love: Helping the Sexual Addict, Dr. Patrick Carnes, Hazelden, 1994

Don't Call It Love: Recovery from Sexual Addiction, Dr. Patrick Carnes, Bantam, 1991

Waking the Dead: The Glory of a Heart Fully Alive, John Eldredge, Thomas Nelson, 2003

Sex God: Exploring the Endless Connections between Sexuality and Spirituality, Rob Bell, Zondervan, 2007

Flesh: An Unbreakable Habit of Purity in a Pornographic World: Men's Edition, Rick James, WSN Press, 2004

Fantasy: An Insatiable Desire for a Satisfying Love: Women's Edition, Betty Blake Churchill with Rick James, CruPress, 2005

RECOVERY GROUPS, SOFTWARE, AND OTHER RESOURCES

<u>Sexual Addiction Twelve-Step Groups</u>

Sexaholics Anonymous (SA)

PO Box 3565

Brentwood, TN 37024

Web site: www.sa.org

E-mail: saico@sa.org

Phone: 615-370-6062

Sex Addicts Anonymous (SAA)

ISO of SAA

PO Box 70949

Houston, TX 77270

Web site: www.saa-recovery.org

E-mail: info@saa-recovery.org

Phone: 713-869-4902

Sex and Love Addicts Anonymous (SLAA)

Fellowship-Wide Services

1550 NE Loop 410, Ste 118

San Antonio, TX 78209

Web site: www.slaafws.org

Phone: 210-828-7900

<u>Faith-based Recovery Groups</u>

Celebrate Recovery

25422 Trabuco Rd #105-151

Lake Forest, CA 92630

Web site: www.celebraterecovery.com

Phone: 949-581-0548

Bethesda Workshops

3710 Franklin Rd
Nashville, TN 37204
Web site: www.bethesdaworkshops.org
E-mail: mferree@bethesdaworkshops.org
Phone: 866-464-4325

L.I.F.E. Ministries / LIFE Groups

PO Box 952317
Lake Mary, FL 32795
Web site: www.freedomeveryday.org
E-mail: info@freedomeveryday.org
Phone: 866-408-LIFE

Internet Filtering and Accountability Tools

Covenant Eyes

1525 W King St
Owosso, MI 48867
Web site: www.covenanteyes.com
E-mail: info@covenanteyes.com
Phone: 877-479-1119

Net Nanny

2369 West Orton Cir
Salt Lake City, UT 84119
Web site: www.netnanny.com
E-mail: info@contentwatch.com
Phone: 801-977-7777

Bsafe Online

PO Box 1819

Bristol, TN 37621

Web site: www.bsafehome.com

Phone: 850-362-4310

Pure Online

660 Preston Forest Center

Dallas, TX 75230

Web site: www.pureonline.com

E-mail: support@anonymous.com

Phone: 214-580-2000

Other Helpful Resources

Brave Hearts

www.bravehearts.net

Porn Nation

www.pornnation.org

Online Sexual Addiction Screening Test Call

www.mysexsurvey.com

SexHelp.com

www.sexhelp.com

ACKNOWLEDGMENTS

My thanks to my dear friend Regi, the very first "brave heart," for supporting me and this mission from day one and convincing me this book needed to be written; to Andy, my pastor, for giving me the confidence to believe I could write it myself; to my boys, Chris and Andrew, for their unconditional love, encouragement, and support; to their mom, my ex-wife, Patty, for contributing her personal journal; to "The Band"—Nick, Rick, Tony, and Ben—for teaching me how to tell my story well; to my sister Cathy and the many other "Writing Sherpas" who showed me the way; to my friend Keith for holding me accountable; to my agent David and his incredible staff for patiently waiting and always believing in me; to my copyeditor and proofreader Elizabeth for making me look better on paper than I really am; to my many, many friends and supporters at Campus Crusade for Christ and North Point Community Church—you're all amazing; to my new friends at Moody Publishers for sharing my passion to reach the nations; to the more than 40,000 college students on campuses throughout the world who have attended our "Porn Nation" events to hear my story—you inspire me and give me great confidence in our future; and finally, to my best friend and beloved wife Christine, who sacrificed more than anyone will ever know so that this book could be written. "I will never leave nor forsake thee."

ABOUT THE AUTHOR

Michael Leahy is a recovering sex addict and the founder and executive director of BraveHearts, an organization dedicated to increasing the public's awareness of the hidden dangers and long-term consequences of pornography consumption. Before launching Brave-Hearts in 2003, Michael was a sales executive in the computer industry and worked for companies like IBM, Unisys, and NEC. Michael is the father of two boys; his first marriage ended in divorce in 1998 after his thirty-year relationship with pornography escalated into a self-destructive sexual addiction.

Now ten years into recovery, Michael has appeared on numerous national television programs like ABC's 20/20 and *The View* and in major media publications such as *USA Today* as an expert on the subjects of pornography, sexual addiction, and the impact sex in media is having on our culture. He's shared his compelling story and expertise in churches, at conferences, and with over 40,000 students on more than one-hundred campuses worldwide in his critically acclaimed multimedia presentation "Porn Nation: The Naked Truth." Michael is remarried and currently resides with his wife, Christine, in the Washington D.C. area.